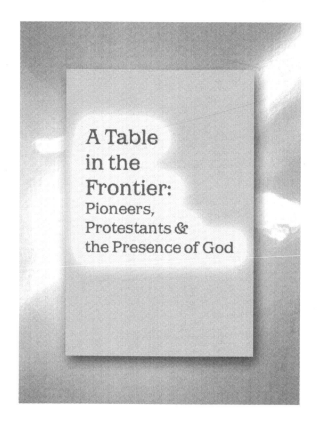

A Table
in the
Frontier:
Pioneers,
Protestants &
the Presence of God

Glenda Orme Clark

Beverly, Chandra, and Karen-
Thank you for being the midwives
that assisted in the birthing of this baby!
I could not have done it without you.

Don-
God has granted you great wisdom.
Thank you for sharing it with me.

May every minute we have invested in this book
represent a thousand souls
ushered into the Kingdom of God!

"Let us come to Him
with large desires,
with great demands,
for He is a great God who will give us
more than even we can cry out for,
even more than we can see
to seek or understand.
And do you say,
'How long shall we cry out for more?'
Until the Heavens open
and He pours down torrents
of His living water upon us."

A quote from Rev. James McGready from 1798.

Dedication

I would be remiss if I did not acknowledge and honor the men that were mightily used of God in the Second Great Awakening: Reverends James McGready, Barton Stone, the McGee brothers (William and John) and Francis Asbury, the first bishop of the Methodist church in America.

In addition to that noble company, are each and every one of the men- a virtually nameless and faceless brotherhood- that Bishop Asbury sent forth into what were dangerous frontiers, carrying the Word of God, and little else and who became the esteemed company of men called the Methodist circuit riders.

With a grateful heart, I dedicate this book to my mother's father, David Groover, who had both Methodist preachers and circuit riders in his lineage. This was a man who loved the Word of God and treasured the singing of hymns. One of the joys of his life was being the song leader for the little Methodist church in Flintville, Tennessee. He faithfully honored the tradition of Shape Note singing, which was first introduced in 1801 to facilitate community singing at the camp meetings.

My earliest memory of him was his voice raised in song early on Sunday mornings in my grandparent's home when our family was visiting. The magnitude of his love for the songs of Zion defies any description I could attempt. He is happily at home in the land of delights, still singing on.

Joining my grandfather is my dad, Raymond Aubrey Pursell, who loved singing hymns almost as much. As I was in the process of completing this book, I remembered that my sweet Daddy was the first person who ever told me about a miracle when I was a child. It was regarding his father, Raymond Roy Pursell, who walked with God, and was quite literally raised from the dead. As I was growing to adulthood, my Dad shared the amazing testimonies of many more miracles. Mine is a multi-generational legacy of faith. After all, when you hear someone in your family was raised from the dead, what seems too hard for God after that?

And, last but certainly not least, to my beloved son, Justin. Even as a very young child you perceived some deep spiritual truths through your dreams. An astounding adventure awaits you, so far beyond anything you can fathom! I consider you to be a 'Son of Thunder' for this generation. You are honest and compassionate, with an extreme sense of both justice and honor. I am grateful to be your mother every day of my life, and I am so very thankful for the beautiful wife God has given you in my sweet Tricia.

As I look back at your life, it is no coincidence that an early nickname for you- given by the father of a family that you loved so dearly- was 'Justin, the prophet'. The call on your life is sure. And, it is for you and your generation that this book is written. May what your eyes see and what your ears hear far exceed anything that is documented in this book!

"O, Flame of Life, Fire of Love,
breathe on me.
Divine Goodness,
Overpowering Sweetness,
open my eyes that I may see You
in the beauty of Your holiness.
Grant vision,
O, Fount of loveliness,
to a blind beggar who has never truly seen.
Bread of Heaven,
feed me, until all of me
is You.
O, Living Water, clean and pure,
quench my desperate thirst,
which spans generations.

I thirst for whatever holy cordial
those that went before me left untasted.
I hunger for any sacred morsel-
for whatever reason- they left behind.
Give to me, O, Tree of Life,
That which was apportioned to them,
residing still somewhere in the Spirit,
that I may eat and drink for them
and be filled,
for I bear them wherever I go."

Glenda Orme Clark

Table of Contents

SECTION FOUR: WHAT THEY SAW & HEARD

SECTION FIVE: HOW SOME WERE IMPACTED

SECTION SIX: REVIVALISTS VS ANTI-REVIVALISTS

SECTION SEVEN: FUTURE AWAKENING PROPHECY

Preface

When I began this project, the focus of my search was simply to know more about some events where the fire of God burned in Goodlettsville, Tennessee (the city where I live) during the early days of the Second Great Awakening. The details came to me slowly as I casually began to research this subject. The truth is I never considered writing a book for others to read. It began as a personal search exclusively because of my desire to know more about what happened here during the early 1800's, and also to see another awakening come to my region, to America and to the world.

I never expected that a simple search would initiate a type of metamorphosis in my own heart. The more I discovered, the more I wanted to know. One piece of information led me to another, until I woke up one day and realized that the project resembled a book more than just an historical paper. This scaffolding surprised even me. It was as if the knowledge of the events I gathered only increased the hunger within me.

The understanding I have gained is both personal and sacred to me. My own life has been deeply impacted by reading the first-hand accounts of those who attended these camp meetings of about two hundred and fifteen years ago. In a sense, those I have researched the most became almost like friends of mine. Somewhere in my mind I know that is not possible, but in an entirely different place inside me, it makes perfect sense.

They are, after all, brothers in the Lord that I have never had the pleasure of meeting…yet.

As I read the testimonies and the details of all of these occasions; I began to see pieces of a puzzle which, I believe, can potentially draw another spiritual awakening for this generation.

What is the most important thing I have learned in the process? Simply put, I now view the celebration of Communion (The Lord's Supper) in an entirely different manner. So much so, that recently when my own church shared Communion together as people sat in their seats, it was almost shocking to me when I placed it over the grid of what I had learned about how it was celebrated in those days of long ago.

Then, as opposed to now, it took days (not minutes) just to prepare to receive Communion. Crowds of people spent multiple days camping together, singing together, praying together, and repenting together. They listened to sermon after sermon with the intention of preparing their hearts to sit at an actual table together in shifts and partake of the elements together in a most holy setting. Each one had to prove their commitment to the Lord in order to receive a metal token with a seat number. This proof of devotion allowed them to join in this sacred occasion.

The entire focus of these meetings revolved around preparing for, and celebrating Communion together. This type of event, called a sacramental service, was the catalyst that ushered in the Presence of God which you will read about in the pages that follow. I appreciate the influence of those of Scots-Irish descent who brought the tradition for these holy occasions to America (from Scotland). We, as believers, owe them a debt of honor.

Even a casual research of events such as these which happened in Scotland as early as the 1600's and 1700's (i.e., Cambuslang* & Shotts) was having much the same shocking physical reactions among the people, as these you will read about in Kentucky and Tennessee. Another important piece of the puzzle is that-separate and apart from a revelation from God- we absolutely cannot comprehend the spiritual condition of our own heart. We have no way of understanding how far away from God we have moved, until He comes among us and opens our eyes. But, when He comes we can see clearly, and then, somehow repentance is not so difficult. God is holy; we – not so much.

In order to birth and maintain a revival awakening it is imperative to have a strong emphasis on a properly celebrated Communion: one where it is not merely a memorial, but a holy feast where God's people renew their covenant with Him. His Presence will come! Can you think of even one occasion when the children of Israel repented and renewed covenant that He did not come?

This book you are holding in your hands is not what some would consider a regular book. It is not me waxing eloquent on how much I know about the dynamics of a spiritual awakening. If it was, it would have been a *very* short book! This is a compilation of many accounts, from many diverse voices. These accounts will serve to document the events of the Second Great Awakening from the perspective of those that lived through it. Long story short, this is the type of book that I would have wanted to read when I began this adventure. It includes eye witness accounts of each event and sometimes even testimonies of how the individuals were impacted by those events. Few things are as powerful as first-hand accounts, and I will include plenty!

I enjoy researching much like a treasure hunter loves digging for treasure, but no one need confuse me with a scholarly researcher, or well accomplished writer. However, it is my hope that I have done this subject justice. It is my sincere belief that words are so very powerful. When heaven breathes on them, they can bring revolutionary change! Harriet Beecher Stowe's book, *Uncle Tom's Cabin*, became a catalyst to end slavery because her words were ordained. Inspired words can awaken the conscience of a person or even a nation. That is the essence of my prayer for this book. I am greatly encouraged that since God can speak through a donkey when necessary, He can do whatever He wants to get the word out! He will use whoever is available!

In a real sense, I have been so completely submerged in the details and minutia of the Second Great Awakening that I have possibly overwhelmed those close to me with all that I have learned in this process. For that, I sincerely apologize. The driving force of this process has been my passionate desire to both honor those that I have read about, and that my own heart would be prepared when awakening comes to my generation.

As you read this book, may you experience an extreme hunger for a visitation from the Lord, and may our collective longing for the Presence of God be so intense and so overwhelming that it will draw Heaven to touch Earth…again.

Glenda Orme Clark
March 24, 2016

"The crown has fallen from our head:
woe to us, we have sinned!
For this our heart is faint,
for these things our eyes are dim...
You, LORD*, remain forever;
Your throne is from generation to generation.
Why do You forget us forever,
forsake us for so long?
Turn us to You, LORD*, and we will be turned.
Renew our days of old."

Lamentations 5: 16, 17, 19-21
One New Man Bible

CHAPTER 1

 The Perspective of Now

Before giving you a historical perspective for the setting of the Second Great Awakening in the late 1700's and early 1800's, it seems appropriate to describe the current landscape of culture so that any similarities can be noted.

We are on a rapid descent as a society; as we stand perilously close to judgement, and we don't even recognize it!

Society is deteriorating. There is a purposeful dismantling of the God-ordained definition of marriage between a man and a woman. The daily sacrifice of thousands of innocent lives is both celebrated and promoted under the banner of the advancement of women's rights. Our very identity as individuals seems to be based more on personal preferences than reality, and gender lines are not only blurred, but non-existent.

These are just a few of the indications that we are in the midst of some very dark days in our own generation. This is the perfect, fertile environment for an abundant harvest of chaos.

Is there anything new under the sun? In Jeremiah 19:5, ancient Israelites literally shocked God with their callous depravity. What were their offenses? In essence, they not only allowed themselves to be influenced by the ungodly culture surrounding them, but they also participated in what were the commonly accepted pagan practices of that time in history.

What were some of those practices that brought judgement?

To begin with, there was an inordinate elevation of women credited to the worship of false goddesses. Children were sacrificed by their willing parents in the fire as an offering to a false god of the day. Of ultimate importance was the issue of a no-holds-barred sexual freedom of expression with perversion being pervasive. Even prostitution (both male and female) was an accepted form of worship in the temples of false gods. In the 8th chapter of Ezekiel, the Lord showed Ezekiel how pagan practices were secretly being done in the very place dedicated to worship of the one true God. That brings to mind an important word. Syncretism is the attempt to combine two things that are diametrically opposed, in this case the sacred and the profane.

From this sort of perverted worship came the conception of unwanted babies. Child sacrifice was utilized as an acceptable solution to what became the unwelcome byproduct of sin.

Fast forward to today. How culturally similar are the current issues of women's rights/radical feminism, abortion and sexual freedom? All three are visibly acceptable to a massive sect of our society daily. And, the root of all three is found in paganism.

For example, to comprehend the reality of child sacrifice in our day, we must come face to face with the enormity of the number of lives that have been lost. In excess of 58.7 million babies have been aborted in America since 1973. (The entire population of South Africa is only around 55 million.) So that means 58 million human beings have been sacrificed in America on the altar of convenience from 1973 to 2016. Every city, every state and most families have been impacted. The loss to our society is palpable.

The unrestrained sexual permissiveness of our time continually produces the same annoying problem: life. Abortion continues to be a culturally acceptable solution to that dilemma, along with the potential to benefit or profit from the harvested organs and tissue of the victims. The only conceivable way that kind of loss can be explained is that our country has lost its collective conscience.

Unbelievably, it is a popular thought within our world to accept the concept that all gods are the same. Claims are made to say that there is only one God, and we call him by the different names of other gods. Temples dedicated to false gods are everywhere, as the rest of us bow down to the god of tolerance.

Even a cursory study of the attributes of those that are considered to be gods by the various religions of our day reveal that they share virtually nothing in common with the God of Abraham, Isaac, and Jacob. It is an age-old story repeating itself.

Distortions abound. Consider your very first thought when you see a painted rainbow on a sign or building. Do you think of the symbol of a promise made by the God of Noah that the earth would never again be destroyed again by water or an illuminated White House that is celebrating the passage of homosexual marriage?

In our generation, we have witnessed the legalization of abortion, sodomy, and adultery. Previous generations were all prohibited of these acts by law. We have without a doubt lost our ability to be shocked as both individuals, and as a nation.

Ok, point made. Now where do we go from here?

The good news is there has never been a dark time in the history of America when we, as a country, were in the midst of a swift downward spiral- much like we are now- that God has not, in His great mercy, brought a spiritual awakening to that generation.

Each and every time this mercy has come, along with it has come the opportunity to turn our hearts back to Him and to redeem and restore our culture by the coming of the Kingdom of God.

When the merciful wake-up call came to a generation, many were shaken awake, and their eyes were opened to see the ugliness of their sin. The call brought about repentance, which in turn put out a welcome mat for the Presence of God.

So here we are, in a land where idols- both personal and cultural- abound, and where we see no problem participating in the ungodly practices of our culture. There seems to be no issue with combining the worship of the idols of our culture with our worship of the one True God. (Does any of this sound familiar?)

In the pages that follow we will observe the steps of our forefathers. We will witness the decline of their culture, and retrace the passion and repentance that propelled them into their Great Awakening.

We have one advantage they didn't have. They have modeled for us the enormous power of united prayers of desperation and genuine, heart-rending repentance.

Can we learn from their example? If not, are we prepared to face the consequences of our actions as individuals, and as a nation?

"In every generation,
man must look upon himself
as if he personally
had gone up out of Egypt."

Ancient Jewish dictum.

CHAPTER 2

 Historical Context

Author's Note: Throughout the content of this book, when you encounter the following terms, "west" and "southwest", those will indicate the physical location of both Southern Kentucky and Northern Tennessee in relation to the original thirteen states in the late 1700's and early 1800's.

The Second Great Awakening which began in the late 1790's was actually preceded by another move of God. The First Great Awakening began in the 1730's and continued until 1743, preceding the American Revolution (1775-1783). As incredible as it may seem, there was a marked spiritual decline even after all of the momentous events of the First Awakening. Many factors brought about this spiritual bankruptcy: the devastation and disillusionment that followed the Revolutionary War, the prevalence of Deism, French Infidelity, Unitarianism, and Universalism. These popular secular schools of thought of that time made a deep impression on the minds of the population in both the established states and the frontier lands of America. (See Historical Terms Defined section for descriptions of the above mentioned schools of thought.)

The following reports will present the historical factors that came into play in the periods of time before, during and after The Second Great Awakening.

<u>Report #1</u>: The First Awakening impacts both Europe and the American colonies.

"The Great Awakening, called by historians the First Great Awakening, was an evangelical and revitalization movement that swept Protestant Europe and British America, and especially the American colonies in the 1730s and 1740s, leaving a permanent impact on American Protestantism. It resulted from powerful preaching that gave listeners a sense of deep personal revelation of their need of salvation by Jesus Christ. Pulling away from ritual, ceremony, sacramentalism and hierarchy, the Great Awakening made Christianity intensely personal to the average person by fostering a deep sense of spiritual conviction and redemption, and by encouraging introspection and a commitment to a new standard of personal morality." [1]

<u>Report #2</u>: Spiritual decline and deadness precedes the Second Awakening.

According to Thomas H. Kiker, "A continent had experienced a great revival early in the eighteenth century, and a new nation had risen up and won its freedom toward the end of the century. One might think that the spiritual climate of the nation would be fervent and thankful. [J. Edwin] Orr writes, 'Yet before the nineteenth century with all its achievements began, there was a desperate death of spiritual life in the areas so recently blessed in revival. The time following the Revolutionary War and continuing through the vast remainder of the eighteenth century was one marked with spiritual apathy.' William Sweet describes it as follows: 'The decade and a half following the close of the American Revolution was one of spiritual deadness among all American churches.'" [2]

<u>Report #3:</u> Lawlessness and spiritual adultery.

"The only period in our history comparable in any way with this present day was out on the western frontier in the period after the Revolution. The frontier at that time was mainly Ohio, Kentucky, and Tennessee. Many areas of the frontier had a reputation for great lawlessness, and at that time, it had few ministers. Indeed, the spiritual condition of the entire country seems to have suffered as a result of the Revolutionary War and also as a result of the influence of Deism, Unitarianism, and the anti-Christian aspects of the French Revolution. Deism is a belief that there is a god, but that He is an impersonal one who has no care or concern for his creation. Many Americans were concerned about the religious state of the nation." [3]

J. Parnell McCarter states, "More than 15,000 of the 300,000 confirmed alcoholics in America died each year. Profanity was rampant, and women were afraid to go outdoors at night for fear of assault and/or rape. Bank robbery, fraud, infidelity, gambling, and licentiousness were common place". [4]

<u>Report #4:</u> Deism further defined.

"Deism paid tribute to the supposed inherent goodness of man and incited lawlessness, self-indulgence, and immorality. [5] At one point, conditions got so bad in America that the French infidel and atheist Voltaire said Christianity would be forgotten in the new nation within three decades. [6]

<u>Report #5:</u> Influence of the secularization of France on America.

According to revival chronicler, J. Edwin Orr, "[In] 1792 moral decline set in following America's War of Independence. As

Frenchmen donated millions of francs to propagandize Americans, Yale president Timothy Dwight bewailed that the dregs of infidelity had been vomited upon the nation. Out of five million people, 300,000 were drunkards, and increased sexual license boosted illegitimacy and venereal diseases.

In the Christian colleges, revolutionary doctrines promoted unrestrained indulgence. The college church was almost as extinct as gambling, intemperance, profanity, and licentiousness thrived. Christians on campus were so few and unpopular that they met in secret to avoid mistreatment. Students burned buildings, forced presidents to resign, destroyed Bibles, and profaned public worship.

The infidelity of the French Revolution posed the greatest challenge to Christianity since the pre-Constantine era. Never had so great a threat lashed against the foundations of the faith, against believing in the God revealed in Scripture." [7]

Report #6: Progression of the great decline in morality.

"Timothy Dwight, the grandson of Jonathan Edwards, described the period before and during the American Revolution:

'The profanation of the Sabbath . . . profaneness of language, drunkenness, gambling, and lewdness, were exceedingly increased; and, what is less commonly remarked, but is not less mischievous, than any of them, a light, vain method of thinking, concerning sacred things, a cold, contemptuous indifference toward every moral and religious subject.'" [8]

Report #7: The end of Christianity?

One church historian wrote: "It seemed as if Christianity was about to be ushered out of the affairs of men." [9]

Report #8: The great push toward the frontier.

As Kevin Wandrei describes it, "Before the year 1800, most of the population of the United States lived on the eastern seaboard of North America. In the early 1800's, however, many Americans began to move west.

The first region west of the original thirteen states that were heavily settled was the Appalachian mountain region, including Tennessee and Kentucky. Unlike other parts of the United States, the Appalachian region was largely populated by Scots-Irish immigrants. This contributed to the region's distinct culture, which includes Celtic-influenced country music. Though Kentucky and Tennessee were admitted to the Union in 1792 and 1796 respectively, their populations did not grow heavily until a decade later.

By the year 1800, 10% of all American citizens lived west of the Appalachian Mountains in Tennessee, Kentucky and parts of modern-day West Virginia." [10]

Report #9: A united cry for awakening is raised up.

There are many reports from the late 1700's where both individuals and groups in many of the original thirteen states entered into covenants to begin to join together to fast and pray for God to bring a spiritual awakening to America.

Many believed that America had declined so severely that the condition was beyond redemption. Still others would accept nothing less than a genuine move of God to restore and redeem what had been lost.

Report #10: A concerted prayer movement arises.

According to J. Edwin Orr, "How did the situation change? It came through a concert of prayer…

Is this not what is missing so much from all our evangelistic efforts: explicit agreement, visible unity, unusual prayer?

This movement had started in Britain through William Carey, Andrew Fuller, John Sutcliffe, and other leaders who began what the British called the Union of Prayer. Hence, the year after John Wesley died (he died in 1791), the Second Great Awakening began and swept Great Britain.

In New England, there was a man of prayer named Isaac Backus, a Baptist pastor, who in 1794, when conditions were at their worst, addressed an urgent plea for prayer for revival to pastors of every Christian denomination in the United States.

Churches knew that their backs were to the wall. All the churches adopted the plan until America, like Britain, was interlaced with a network of prayer meetings, which set aside the first Monday of each month to pray. It was not long before revival came." [11]

Report #11: Spiritual hunger of individuals precedes awakening.

"The Great Revival [The Second Great Awakening] lasted about five to seven years, depending on what year you count as its beginning.

It is generally held to have begun in the year of our Lord 1800, but some of the local people placed its beginnings even earlier. Some place its origin as far back as 1797. (*Early Times in Middle Tennessee*, Carr.)

As early as 1797, grown men, members of one or another of James McGready's three little churches were spending days at a time in the woods, under deep conviction, praying, crying, weeping, and seeking God for an assurance of their personal salvation.

In some writings of James McGready's published in 1837, some twenty years after his death, and appropriately titled, *The Posthumous Works of James McGready*, McGready spoke of an 'awakening' among his congregations beginning in 1797, during the spring following his arrival in Logan County. He goes on to say, "But the year 1800 exceeds all that my eyes ever beheld on earth." [12]

"The rough, violent, irreligious frontier,
which many felt threatened
to undo the morals of the new nation,
was being tamed
by the Lamb of God."

The Return of the Spirit
Christian History Institute

CHAPTER 3

 Cultural Context - Kentucky

In the late 1700's and early 1800's, southern Kentucky was an oasis and a stronghold for hardened criminals of every variety. To say anarchy and chaos reigned supreme in that location is a complete understatement.

The following reports will bear witness to the dire spiritual atmosphere of Kentucky:

Report #1: Morals on the frontier were almost non-existent.

According to historian Paul Dienstberger, "What arrived in the West was the biggest collection of lawbreakers, whiskey drinkers, and the most uncontrolled lot in the world. Morals were non-existent. Few women were Christians and even fewer men admitted their faith... The West was considered the most profane place in all Christendom, and the only standards of judgement were the gun and 'Lynch's Law', the rope. But, death and danger were threats from an arrow, or milk sickness or even some wounded animal.'

One of the most infamous areas of this region was Logan County, Kentucky. It was known as...[Satan's Stronghold]... because of lawlessness, gambling, drunkenness, and immorality. Residents of the community pledged to keep out any form of official law enforcement and civil order." [13]

<u>Report #2:</u> Cruelty the pioneers experienced on the frontier.

A. H. Redford states, "In Kentucky, the ambitious came to carve out their homes from the kingly forests of the fresh and untouched wilderness. The settlement of Kentucky by the Anglo-American pioneer was no easy task. The fierce and merciless savage stubbornly disputed the right to the soil. The attempt to locate upon these rich and fertile lands was a proclamation of war: of [a] war whose conflict should be more cruel than had been known in all the bloody pages of the past. On his captive the Indian inflicted the most relentless torture: Neither the innocence of infancy, the tears of beauty, nor the decrepitude of age could awaken his sympathy or touch his heart. The tomahawk and the stake were the instruments of his cruelty. But notwithstanding the dangers that constantly imperiled the settlers, attracted by the glowing accounts of the beauty of the country and the fertility of the soil, brave hearts were found that were willing to leave their patrimonial homes in Carolina and Virginia, and hazard their lives amid the flowing forests of the West." [14]

<u>Report #3:</u> Greed for land drove some toward the frontier.

"Many of the socio-religious conditions in Kentucky mirrored those of the country in general in post-revolutionary America. [Rev. James] McGready complained that Kentuckians were worldly people whose conversations were 'of corn and tobacco, or land and stock…. the name of Jesus has no charms; it is rarely mentioned unless to be profaned.' Indeed, the rush for land represented a change in post-war demographics that were perhaps nowhere as dramatic as in Kentucky. In 1790, the population was about 73,000, roughly sixteen percent of whom were slaves, with most of the population concentrated in the central Bluegrass area near Lexington. By 1800, the population had almost tripled to 221,000, and had expanded farther west, spurred by the decisive Battle of Fallen Timbers in 1794. This defeat of confederated Indian tribes near Toledo, Ohio, by General Anthony Wayne, effectively ended the threat of Indian attack in Kentucky by the middle of the decade. Though people of all classes came to Kentucky, the influx of large numbers of the poor in search of land produced a dramatic effect on the country as a whole. The 1800 United States Census revealed that seven percent of the United States population lived west of the Alleghenies in what is now Kentucky, Tennessee and Ohio.

By 1810, the population in Kentucky had swelled to almost double that of 1800, to 406,000." [15]

Report #4: Lawlessness prevailed.

J. Edwin Orr states, "Congress had discovered that in Kentucky there had not been more than one court of justice held in five years. Peter Cartwright, Methodist evangelist, wrote that when his father settled in Logan County, it was known as Rogues' Harbor. If someone committed a murder in Massachusetts or robbery in Rhode Island, all he needed to do was to cross the Alleghenies. The decent people in Kentucky formed regiments of vigilantes to fight for law and order, fought a pitched battle with outlaws and lost." [16]

Report #5: Tears prepare the way for a spiritual awakening.

"[Rev. James] McGready settled in Logan County [KY], pastor of three little churches. He wrote in his diary that the winter of 1799 for the most part was 'weeping and mourning with the people of God.' Lawlessness prevailed everywhere." [17]

Report #6: Religious indifference abounds.

"Five years earlier [before Cane Ridge revival in 1801], few would have predicted the Cane Ridge [KY] revival. Since the American Revolution, Christianity had been on the decline, especially on the frontier. Sporadic, scattered revivals- in Virginia in 1787/88, for example, dotted the landscape, but they were short-lived. Religious indifference seemed to be spreading." [18]

Report #7: The perfect setting for a move of God.

"In 1795 the Reverend James Smith, a Methodist passing through Kentucky, noted that the infidels in the region had 'given Christianity a deadly stab.' But, 'the Lord hath his way in the wilderness and all things obey his might.' I trust he will yet bring good out of this evil, and that the glory of scriptural religion, [though] obscure for the present, will shine forth with redoubled luster." [19]

Report #8: Hope for change is rekindled.

As noted revival historian John B. Boles states, "At the close of the eighteenth century, Kentucky, with the rest of the South, had reached the point where dozens of ministers and thousands of church members were convinced that God would someday send his glorious deliverance. Prayer societies, fasts, intense and urgent sermons, all were united in an effort to bring men into the necessary relationship with God. Hopeful expectation had largely subdued ministerial pessimism. Throughout the South, from the sea islands of South Carolina to the piedmont of Virginia, and even to the 'Barrens' of Kentucky, the faithful remnant was waiting for God to send a revival.

None could be sure where or when it would start, but all could be sure of one thing: God would do his work in strange and wonderful ways. This miraculous manifestation would be the seal, proving the authenticity of the heaven-sent revival." [20]

Report #9: The faithful hear the call to pray.

"'There was never a time,' wrote the Reverend Robert Wilson in 1793, 'in which so many young men were turning to the ministry…makes me think one of two things will inevitably follow–either they will be dispised [despised] & loaded with reproaches from every quarter, or they will be instruments in the hand of God in producing a glorious revival.'" [21]

"Five of these young licentiates who shared the evangelistic zeal and theology [tripartite theology of repentance, faith, and regeneration] of their mentor [James McGready] subsequently migrated to Kentucky, there to play an indispensable role in the development of the Great Revival: William McGee, Barton W. Stone, William Hodge, Samuel McAdow, and John Rankin." [22] [Each of these men participated in the camp meeting revivals which later swept across Kentucky and Tennessee, along with other states.]

CHAPTER 4

 Cultural Context - Tennessee

When the stirrings of revival first visited Tennessee, it was a frontier, pure and simple. It was full of the type of people (fiercely independent pioneer stock!) that were willing to face danger and hardship to carve out a new life for their families. This type of adventure was not for the faint of heart. Due to disease, and the opposition they faced at the hands of the Native Americans, many did not survive long in the frontier. Those who did were powerfully impacted by the frequent loss of loved ones (even children), by sickness and many times due to violent deaths at the hands of warriors. Early on, those who risked their lives realized the tremendous cost of planting lives in the frontier.

The following reports will paint an accurate picture of frontier life in what would become the state of Tennessee.

Report #1: Tennesseans, a rowdy melting pot of pioneers.

Author Wilma Dykeman offers this insight, "There were many English, some Germans – mainly from the Palatinate – and Welsh and Irish, a few Huguenots; the dominant character of Tennesseans came to be identified with that of the Scots-Irish. Fondness for migration was only one of their characteristics.

Tennessee historian John Trotwood Moore listed others: 'If abused, they fight; if their rights are infringed, they rebel; if forced, they strike; and if their liberties are threatened, they murder. They eat meat and always like their bread hot.'" [23]

Report #2: The great push for land.

"On a trip to Tennessee in 1794, Methodist Bishop Francis Asbury wrote anxiously about frontier settlers, 'When I reflect that not one in a hundred came here to get religion, but rather to get plenty of good land, I think it will be well if some or many do not eventually lose their souls.'" [24]

Report #3: Tennesseans love Tennessee!

"Tennesseans, even at their most rebellious, have tended to bear a strong allegiance to their place. Perhaps this sense was embedded early and firmly in the fact that, for long generations, Tennesseans were outdoor people. This was true not only for the hunters, trappers, surveyors, farmers, lumbermen, but for most of the professionals as well. Preachers 'pastored' several churches, or followed arduous circuits in their struggle to tame the unfettered spirits of a civilization-in-the-shaping…

There have been many jokes about this sense of place and Tennesseans… One story…involves a man who died and went to heaven. All was beautiful and as he'd expected – except for one large group of people who were chained to trees. The newcomer asked who these people were, and St. Peter replied, 'Those are Tennesseans. It's Friday, and we have to chain them to keep them from going back home for the weekend.'" [25]

Report #4: Tenacious volunteers.

"Thus, protesting, separating, revolting, and believing, laboring, enduring, Tennesseans found and built their place. If their geography represented a wedding of opposites, so, too, did their character.

Many of them were farmers who hated wars, and suspected any standing army, but they did not shun a fight. Indeed, their very name- the Volunteers- reflects the readiness with which ordinary citizens rallied to the call to arms…" [26]

Report #5: The prevalence of secular beliefs of the time.

"Andrew Fulton, a Presbyterian missionary from Scotland, discovered in Nashville and in 'all the newly formed towns in this western colony, there are few religious people.' The minutes of the frontier Transylvania Presbytery reveal deep concern about the 'prevalence of vice & infidelity, the great apparent declension of true vital religion in too many places.'

Rampant alcoholism and avaricious land-grabbing were matched by the increasing popularity of both Universalism (the doctrine that all will be saved) and Deism (the belief that God is uninvolved in the world)." [27]

Report #6: Pioneering Tennesseans.

Doug Drake states, "During the year 1788, at least twenty-two families numbering approximately 140 persons came over the mountains to Sumner County. Among those was Andrew Jackson.

Escorted from Southwest Point by Colonel Mansker and Major Kirkpatrick at the head of 100 guardsmen recruited in Davidson and Sumner County, the new settlers carved out ten or twelve new stations [forts] and settled down to the serious business of clearing land and guarding against Indian attack.

The original Cumberland Road was little more than a rough path. In most places it was just wide enough for a single wagon's passage.

It was filled with all the dangers of travel during that era; not the least of which was threat of ambush by the warrior nations. 1792 was the year of greatest depredation along the trace. Well over one hundred settlers lost their lives during this period; many more simply vanished or were unaccounted for." [28]

Report #7: Priorities of early Tennesseans.

"Tennesseans have believed in the gun, the Bible, and themselves – not necessarily in that order, but all together." [29]

Report #8: A blend of diverse people groups.

"The western frontier which would eventually become known as Tennessee attracted them all: seekers after gold and glory; trappers of fur and dealers in the raw, reeking, precious hides; builders of empire; dreamers of a better society wrought in this world and saviors of souls for the next world; speculators making their own laws and rogues fleeing all law; and settlers – always the settlers – scrambling along the narrow trails, hacking out homesteads in the wilderness, clinging tenaciously, ferociously, to their newly won rights of property and liberty. They represented the great proud kingdoms of Europe." [30]

"Come here, admire Christ's love to us,
That gives His Flesh for Food;
And Drink to us He doth provide,
By pouring out His Blood.

This Blood doth Life unto the Dead,
Health to the Sick impart;
This Drink revives the fainting Soul,
And melts the frozen Heart.

What folly is't for men to starve,
Or feed on husks like swine;
When Christ calls to a Table spread,
To feast on food Divine."

18th century Scottish sacramental hymn
by Reverend John Willison, dean and theologian
of the Scottish sacramental revivals.

CHAPTER 5

 Influence of Scots-Irish Sacramentalism

For literally hundreds of years, there has been a strong connection between sacramental occasions (known in our day as Communion or The Lord's Supper) and supernatural encounters with the Presence of the Lord. Originally, these began in Scotland among the Ulster Scots as early as the 1600's and were recreated in America in the early eighteenth century (1700's) when large numbers of the Ulster Scots immigrated to the colonies. The service differs greatly from what is practiced in churches in modern times. The following is a description that will paint a visual picture of what it was like to attend one of these services.

"'I have the happiness to inform you, that the Lord is yet doing wonders in our country,' the Reverend James McGready reported from Logan County, Kentucky in 1803. 'Our sacramental occasions are days of the Son of Man indeed, and are usually marked with the visible footsteps of Jehovah's majesty and glory...[At] the sacrament in the Ridge congregation [Sumner County, TN],...[t]here were upwards of five hundred communicants; at the tables, through the evening, and during the greater part of the night, the people of God were so filled with such extatic [ecstatic] raptures of divine joy and comfort, that I could compare it to nothing else than the New Jerusalem coming down from heaven to earth.'" [31]

As noted author, Leigh Eric Schmidt reports, "Thus did one of America's leading revivalists describe the Pentecostal outpourings during the Great Revival [the Second Great Awakening] that affected a substantial part of the new republic between 1790 and 1810.

At the center of his account stood the sacramental season, a four-day evangelical festival with a long history intertwined from the first with revival. McGready stood near the end of a tradition that had its inception in post-Reformation Scotland; he with many others was a guardian of a set of venerable rituals that had arisen and throve over the past two centuries. The American revivals that he and others like him led take much of their meaning from this long history." [32]

"The sacramental occasions, Willison attested, helped create 'a bond of mutual love and unity among believers themselves'; it was, he said, 'an excellent mean(s) for procuring and advancing unity and love among the saints and servants of God.'" [33]

In order to understand the tremendous weight that McGready [and those of the Presbyterian denomination] placed on the sacramental services they held so dear to their hearts, one must consider a man named Martin Luther and the events of the Reformation in the 1500's that initiated a tsunami of change that would flow from Europe to America.

"Born in Eisleben, Germany, in 1483, Martin Luther went on to become one of Western history's most significant figures. Luther spent his early years in relative anonymity as a monk and scholar. But in 1517 Luther penned a document attacking the Catholic Church's corrupt practice of selling 'indulgences' to absolve sin.

His '95 Theses,' which propounded two central beliefs—that the Bible is the central religious authority and that humans may reach salvation only by their faith and not by their deeds—was to spark the Protestant Reformation. Although these ideas had been advanced before, Martin Luther codified them at a moment in history ripe for religious reformation. The Catholic Church was ever after divided, and the Protestantism [Protestors] that soon emerged was shaped by Luther's ideas. His writings changed the course of religious and cultural history in the West." [34]

In Martin Luther's day in the Catholic Church the Eucharist restricted personal participation to only one time per year. In 1520, he advocated that it should be celebrated daily, which was probably shocking to some. For him, The Lord's Supper was an integral element in official worship in which the people enjoy fellowship in and with Jesus Christ. [35]

"Much of the hostility between the Catholics and Protestants was focused on the celebration of the Eucharist [commonly known in modern times as The Lord's Supper or Communion]. At no point did the Protestant leaders, such as [John] Knox and George Hay, bristle more than at the thought of the Catholic Mass... They were equally, if not more offended by the Catholic notion of transubstantiation [the teaching that the bread and the wine used in the sacrament of the Eucharist become, not merely as by a sign or a figure, but also in actual reality the body and blood of Christ]...which they saw as a carnal misrepresentation of the true mode of Christ's presence in the sacrament. [The Protestant belief was that Christ's presence, mediated through the Holy Spirit, was real [and] the Lord was manifest in the true, divinely instituted performance of 'that mystical action.' At the table the faithful…were made one with him…]" [36]

"In addition to the rejection of the Catholic belief of transubstantiation, the Protestants also took issue with both how this [Communion] was to be celebrated, and how often. The Catholics believed that one receiving the bread must kneel before an administering priest, not touching the bread [or host], not being allowed to receive the cup, and also that the ritual was limited only to certain occasions. The Protestants believed that [both of] the elements should be served regularly and more in the style of 're-creating Christ's Last Supper' as they envisioned the Evangelists [disciples] and Paul receiving it." [37]

"Revivalism, a critical component of the Great Awakening, actually began in the 1620's in Scotland among Presbyterians, and featured itinerant preachers. To this end, they changed the focus of the rite from a sacrificial altar to a Communion table and the standard posture at the reception of the elements from kneeling to sitting. They argued, too, that Christ had not distributed the bread and wine to each of the disciples individually, but that the apostles had divided the elements among themselves. This example, the Scottish reformers believed, ruled out priestly distribution to each of the communicants; instead those seated at the table were to handle the sacred elements themselves, passing the bread and wine from one to another. They also insisted that Christ had intended both the consecrated bread and wine to be shared in by all communicants [and] that the Catholics in allowing the laity the Host [bread] alone were 'stealing from the people…'the blessed cup.'

...they [the Scottish reformers] sought to make lay participation in it [The Lord's Supper] a regular, or at least semi-regular, part of Christian worship... their larger aim of separating lay reception of the Eucharist from Catholic holy days – such as Pasch, Yule, or Good Friday – were more successful. For the reformers, holy days [those previously listed] were superstitious, unwarranted by Scripture, and thus best eliminated.

The reformers sought to end this cycle [of high holy days], to make life a perpetual festivity with Christ.

These evangelicals [a growing group of Presbyterians] seemed prepared to step into the breach created by the elimination of the high days of medieval Catholicism and offer in their stead a great public event centered on the celebration of the Reformed Lord's Supper." [38]

According to John Livingston, "Fast forward to 1630 in Scotland, where some very unusual things happened at one of these Reformed sacramental services. John Livingston was an itinerant Presbyterian preacher [who] arrived for one of his stops at the Kirk of Shotts for the celebration of a 'solemn Communion'. There he joined with a handful of the most popular ministers of the Presbyterians...for a series of meetings that reportedly went on 'almost day and night, for four or five days together'. These highly-charged meetings found culmination on Monday in an extraordinary 'down-pouring of the SPIRIT.' On that Monday, outdoors in 'the Church-yard,' Livingston preached a sermon he always considered the most powerful he every delivered. As he exhorted the 'great multitude...there convened' for two-and-a-half-hours in 'a soft shower of rain,' his words had 'a strange unusual MOTION on the hearers; it was even said that many were so overwhelmed…that they fainted away and laid on the ground 'as if they had been dead.' One chronicler concluded that 'near 500 had, at that time, a discernible change wrought in them… [and] could date either their conversion or some remarkable confirmation in their case, on that day.'… More than any other event, the impressive revival at Shotts indicated that the sacramental occasion had come into its own and was helping foment a Presbyterian awakening." [39]

"The prominence of the Communions of the 1650's, like the salience of the revival at Shotts, has led some historians to credit – or more often blame – the most zealous Presbyterians of this decade with the invention of the sacramental season. 'Church historians are practically unanimous,'…that these mass Communions originated with the Protestors [as the most ardent Presbyterians were then known] in the early 1650's." [This was the origin of the Protestants.] [40]

After arriving in the New World of America, the Scots-Irish Presbyterian leaders and laity continued to celebrate the sacramental services in much the same way that they did in Scotland.

Historical Collections offer this insight, "One example of the transformative power that the act of receiving the elements could hold comes from an account penned in 1757 by the colonial pastor John Wright. He spoke in particular of one communicant whose feelings of unworthiness made him extremely reluctant to come to the table. Though this confused penitent eventually 'accepted a token trembling' and managed to sit down at the table, he did not take a piece of bread when it was passed to him.

Seeing this, Wright confronted him:

'I took the bread and went to him, but he told me that he could feel no faith. 'I dare not take it', said he. 'But don't you want a Saviour', said I? 'O yes, O yes', said he; 'but I am not worthy of him'. 'But are you not needy?' 'O yes', said he, 'I am lost without him'. 'But are you not laboring and heavy laden', said I? 'O yes, O yes', said he, 'I am crushed under the load of sin'. 'Well, then', said I, 'Christ calls you by name to come to him', upon which he took the bread into his hand and stood upright, and being a tall man, all the assembly almost could see him, and stretched forth his hands as far as he could, and looked with the most affecting countenance that ever I saw on the symbol of Christ's body, and wept and prayed to this purpose: 'Lord Jesus, I am lost without thee,' looking intensely at the bread; 'I come trembling; I would fain be a partaker of the broken body, for I am undone without thee; Lord Jesus, have mercy on me.' He then attempted to put the bread into his mouth, but, by the trembling, could hardly get the bread into his mouth. He then sat down, and with all imaginable sedateness, partook of the wine. You would never forget the solemn transaction between Christ and that poor sinner, if you were [a] spectator, as I was. I know I shall never [forget this] in this world, as long as I can remember anything.'

Though no doubt an exceptional case in the form that it took, the spectacular potentialities of the sacramental season are nonetheless altogether clear in a passage like this one... As this man looked at his salvation in 'the symbol of Christ's body,' in turn the congregants – spectators all – watched this 'solemn transaction.'

'The whole day,' Wright concluded, 'was one of the days of the Son of Man when Christ was lifted on the cross; he seemed as if he would draw all unto himself.'

At such moments, sinners and saints saw and experienced transformation through the Presbyterian sacrament." [41]

According to Catharine Caroline Cleveland, "Sacramental occasions and quarterly meetings afforded the best opportunity for reaching the people generally. These were usually well attended, even before the Great Revival, as they furnished an opportunity of meeting friends and hearing the gospel to many who, in their remote cabins, knew no neighborhood life and were out of reach of even the irregular preaching afforded by most western communities at the end of the eighteenth century.

The sacramental meetings were a great feature in such lives. This, the revival leaders were quick to appreciate and take advantage of [the gatherings]. As soon as it became noised about that unusual excitement was to be found at these meetings, great crowds flocked to them. The increased attendance made it necessary to devise some new scheme of entertaining those who came from a distance since the hospitality afforded by the neighborhood was no longer adequate. This resulted in the development of camp meetings which immediately became an important element in religious life and most effectively fostered the revival spirit." [42]

An artist's conception of a sacramental meeting in the frontier.

"Jesus, Thy feast we celebrate;
At Thy command the bread we eat,
And drink the cup of sacred wine:
To show Thy death thy friends combine.
Do this we will, and so prepare
To meet Thee coming in the air.

Thy table shows Thy love and grace,
And entertains our souls with peace:
Our hearts by right are only Thine;
Possess them, Lord, with love divine:
Nail our desires unto the cross;
For all besides Thee is but dross.

Christ made me at His table dine;
He ravished me with love divine;
He gave a taste of future bliss:
I said, He's mine, and I am His;
All treasures here Thou'rt far before:
Since Christ is mine, I ask no more."

Excerpt from an 18th century Scottish sacramental hymn
written by Reverend John Willison.

"It is the good news of God's promise
that no matter how apostate His people become,
revival is [always] possible.

A sinful and apostate nation must repent,
reject idolatry, seek God, and obey His laws and commands.
Obedience and loyalty to the Lord is manifest especially
in the corporate worship and covenant ordinances
of the Mosaic laws."

William L. De Arteaga
Forgotten Power:
The Significance of The Lord's Supper in Revival [43]

CHAPTER 6

 Historical Terms Defined

The following are some definitions for terms used during the Second Great Awakening that we may not be familiar with, may no longer be in use, or the meaning may be entirely different in modern times.

Armenianism – The fundamental principle in Arminianism is the rejection of predestination, and a corresponding affirmation of the freedom of the human will.

Cambuslang – The site of an historic sacramental service near Glasgow, Scotland in 1742 where 30,000+ people came to hear the preaching of George Whitefield and to participate in the sacramental observance.

Camp meeting – a type of religious meeting held outdoors due to very large crowds that could not be accommodated in a building. Very often the crowds spent several days together (5-14) in intense preparation to celebrate the elements of Communion (bread and wine) together.

Communicant – a person who receives or is entitled to receive the elements of Communion (bread and wine).

Communion – the ceremony made up of the elements of bread and wine/grape juice to corporately remember the death of the Lord Jesus Christ.

Communion token – was a small metal coin that would be distributed to those who were able to prove their commitment to God. Used as early as 1586, but primarily in the 1800's.

Cumberland country – was the area of land drained by the Cumberland River and its tributaries.

Deism – a secular school of thought that "denied the reality of God's intervention in the lives of people and rejected any notion of supernatural guidance or answers to prayer… Deism taught that the Bible was a myth, mostly allegory, and full of fables. Inspired revelation from God was thought to be nonexistent or irrelevant". [44]

Exercises – referred to physical manifestations that were often exhibited at camp meetings (shaking, falling, jerking, etc.).

Enthusiasm – to be overtaken with or controlled by emotions [in many cases a negative term] mostly referring to Methodists.

Eucharist – a ceremony commemorating The Last Supper, in which bread and wine are consecrated and consumed. This was also referred to as both Holy Communion and the Sacraments.

Exhorters – those that would speak encouragement to people attending camp meetings who were under the conviction of the Holy Spirit, encouraging them to abandon their lives to God.

First Great Awakening – also referred to as The Great Awakening. Most believe the duration was from 1730 to 1755.

Infidelity – a particularly virulent form of atheism that was imported to America by the French during and after the American Revolutionary War.

Meetinghouse/Meeting House – a term used in referring to a church building. "Church" is used in the Bible to mean the Christians in a local area, a local group of Christians meeting together, or the entire body of Christ throughout creation. Those directly involved in the revival commonly used the term "meetinghouse" when speaking of the building where a local church or congregation met.

Messrs. – 19th century title referring formally to more than one man simultaneously.

Professor – someone who professed to be a Christian; someone who professed to be saved.

Protestors – were proponents of what would become known as Protestants, which was a group of people who separated themselves from the Catholic Church and whose beliefs were shaped by the ideas of Martin Luther during the Reformation. The focus of their 'protest' was primarily in how the sacraments of Communion/Eucharist were celebrated.

Religion – to get or to have religion in 1800 meant to be born again, to be saved, to become a Christian. In the Great Revival, and in the teaching of James McGready and other ministers who favored the revival, anyone who was saved would have a consciousness of it within them. If one did not have this inner witness of the Spirit, they were told to assume that they were unsaved, or "unconverted," without religion.

Sacramental meeting – these were meetings that centered on preparing for (sometimes for days) and the sharing and partaking of the elements of Communion together at a common table.

Second Great Awakening – also referred to as The Great Revival. Most believe the duration was from 1790 to 1840.

Swooning – is to faint under the influence of extreme emotion.

Unitarianism – an expression of rationalistic influences that believed the Bible was a metaphor, that Jesus was a prophet and rejected the notion of the Trinity (Father, Son and Holy Spirit).

Universalism – the belief in universal salvation, that all would be saved with God being too benevolent to condemn anyone to eternal punishment.

West and Southwest – when found in this publication, these terms indicate the physical location of both Southern Kentucky and Northern Tennessee from the perspective of the original thirteen states in the late 1700's and early 1800's.

Witness of the Spirit – an assurance from the Holy Spirit to your inward self that something was true, and generally used to mean a witness that you were saved.

"As to the work in general,
there can be no question,
but it is of God." [45]

Reverend Moses Hoge
in reference to the Cane Ridge meeting in 1801.

CHAPTER 7

 Timeline of Historical Events

1517	Reformation began with Martin Luther.
1560	The ascendancy of Protestantism in Scotland.
1730 - 1755	First Great Awakening in America.
1742- Feb. to Nov.	The Cambuslang Work (Wark), a period of extraordinary religious activity in Cambuslang, Scotland.
1754 - 1763	Duration of the French and Indian War.
1775 - 1783	Duration of the American Revolutionary War.
1787	John Hodge & William McGee preached in Sumner County at a location that became Shiloh Presbyterian Church.
	Reverend Benjamin Ogden was appointed by the Baltimore Conference to be the circuit preacher of the Cumberland Settlement in TN.
	Regular preaching in Sumner County, TN by Ogden, Haw, Massy, Williamson, Lee, McHenry and O'Cull who were the first Methodist preachers to bring the gospel.
	Methodist circuit riding preachers preached to small gatherings at some of the forts and stations in Sumner County, Tennessee.

1788	During this year, at least twenty-two families numbering approximately 140 persons came over the mountains to Sumner County to settle.
1790's - 1840	Second Great Awakening in America.
1790's	West Station Camp congregation (Baptist) had a meetinghouse at a place about halfway between Shackle Island and Cottontown.
1792	Shiloh Presbyterian Church was established. Second Presbyterian church founded in Middle Tennessee. The meetinghouse was on a hill about three miles northwest of Cairo, immediately east of the location later chosen for Gallatin.
	Kentucky becomes 15th state.
1796	Tennessee becomes 16th state.
1798	Beech Presbyterian Church was founded on Drake's Creek with Hugh Kirkpatrick acting as pastor until the arrival of William McGee from Shiloh in 1800.
1799	Land was donated by James Sanders for the first Methodist meetinghouse called Drakes Creek Meetinghouse, located on what is now Sanders Ferry Park in Hendersonville, TN.
June/1800	Red River sacramental meeting where many believe the Second Great Awakening began.
July/1800	Gasper River sacramental meeting, Kentucky.

Summer/1800	A vast multitude of people assembled at a sacramental meeting held at Robert Shaw's on the head waters of Red River.
August/1800	Muddy River sacramental meeting, Kentucky.
Sept./1800	The Ridge Congregation (Sumner County, TN) where a meeting was held.
Sept./1800	Sacramental meeting was held at Blythe's Big Spring on Desha's Creek (Gallatin). This meeting was said to comprise the largest number of people ever known to be collected together in the country [at that time]. [46]
October/1800	The revival commenced in Sumner County, TN (Drakes Creek Meetinghouse), which was the first camp meeting held in Tennessee. And then a series of sacramental meetings or revivals held in the county in 1800 were Sumner's part of 'the great revival' that swept much of the western frontier at that time.
1800	Isaac Walton donated six acres of his land (that was adjacent to Casper Mansker's land in Goodlettsville) to his neighbors for camp meetings and worship.
1800?	Hubbard Saunders (Methodist) was building a log meetinghouse called Saunders Chapel on his farm ten miles from Beech Presbyterian Church meetinghouse. [No relation to James Sanders who donated land for Drake's Creek Meeting House.]

1800?	Rehoboth meetinghouse was built on Cage's Bend by another Methodist congregation.
1800	Strother's meetinghouse was erected by Methodists at Cottontown, TN on land owned by Robert Strother.
Aug./1801	Sacramental Camp Meeting held at Cane Ridge Camp Meeting, KY.
1802	First Methodist Annual Conference was held in Tennessee (west of the Cumberland Mountains) at Strother's Meetinghouse.
1811	Disagreement in the Presbyterian Church over the educational qualifications for their ministers, led to a division in the established Presbyterian Church and the organization of the Cumberland Presbyterian Church.
1812 - 1815	Awakening temporarily interrupted by the War of 1812.

"[The minister] must use every possible means to alarm
and awaken Christ-less sinners from their security
and bring them to a sense of their danger and guilt.
He must use every argument to convince them of the horrors of
an unconverted state; he must tell them the worst of their case –
roar the thunders of Sinai in their ears,
and flash the lightning's of Jehovah's vengeance in their faces…
Let them hear or not, though the world may scorn and revile us,
call us low preachers, and madmen, [or] Methodists –
do this we must, or we will be the worst murderers;
the blood of sinners will be required at our hands–
their damnation will lie at our door." [47]

Reverend James McGready

CHAPTER 8

Leaders of the Second Great Awakening

James McGready, 'Son of Thunder'

"He was favored with great nearness to God
and intimate communion with Him."[48]

Account #1:

Tom Ruley states, "McGready was born about 1760 in Pennsylvania to Scots-Irish Presbyterian parents who moved to North Carolina [Guilford County] in 1778. When he was older, McGready returned to Pennsylvania to study under two Presbyterian evangelists, Joseph Smith and John McMillian [at Log School which was based on William Tennent's Log College], who taught him to be a fiery preacher. In 1788, he returned to North Carolina where his intense preaching met with stiff opposition from the 'better' classes of people whom he charged with hypocrisy, materialism and sin." [49]

Account #2:

According to Edwin J. Orr, his [James McGready's] physical appearance…drew notice:

"There was a Scots-Irish Presbyterian minister named James McGready, whose chief claim to fame was he was so ugly that he attracted attention. It was reported that people sometimes stopped in the street to ask, 'What does he do?' 'He's a preacher.'

Then they reacted, saying, 'A man with a face like that must really have something to say.'" [60]

Account #3:

Revival historian John B. Boles states, "About the year 1790, McGready married and with his bride made his home midway between his two congregations [Haw River and Stoney Creek, Guilford County, North Carolina]. Like most Presbyterian ministers, he soon opened a school in his home. One can easily understand why the young and impressionable students were so affected by McGready.

A very plain dresser, he was a large, rather portly man, six feet tall, with prominent features. His grave appearance and piercing eyes chained one's attention; his voice seemed unearthly, coarse, and tremulous. Thunderous tones and jerky gesticulations increased his hypnotic ability to sway an audience. The preacher usually began very calmly, but as he progressed he increased in tempo, volume, and enthusiasm – his conclusions never failed to be fervent and firey. Especially did he excel in public prayer; congregations were often brought to tears by his long, original, and poignant 'wrestlings with God.'

Barton W. Stone [who was converted under McGready's ministry], later one of the outstanding revivalists in Kentucky, remembered first hearing McGready preach at Caldwell's academy: 'such earnestness, such zeal, such powerful persuasion, enforced by the joys of heaven and miseries of hell, I had never witnessed before. My mind was chained by him, and followed him closely in his rounds of heaven, earth, and hell with feeling indescribable.'

'His concluding remarks were addressed to the sinner to flee the wrath to come without delay. Never before had I comparatively felt the force of truth.

Such was my excitement that, had I been standing, I should have probably sunk to the floor under the impression'". [51]

Account #4:

Another source says, "His zeal provoked opposition. The cry was raised against him that he was running the people distracted, diverting their attention from their necessary avocations, and created unnecessary alarm in the minds of those who were decent and orderly in their lives. A letter was written to him in blood, requiring him to leave the country at the peril of this life; a number of wicked men and women of the baser sort, on a certain occasion during the week, assembled in his church, tore down the seats, set fire to the pulpit, and burnt it to ashes." [52]

Account #5:

"McGready taught that all true revival came from God and must be preceded by prevailing prayer and that with that prevailing prayer, God would send true revival. McGready sought the most 'ungodly, irreligious' place in America, as an area where his teaching on revival could be proven. The spot he chose was a part of Logan County, Kentucky, along Red River...

James McGready got several hundred people, most of them living in North Carolina, to sign his 'Carolina Covenant', promising to pray and intercede with God until such time as He would send true revival to Logan County. These people were asked to pray without ceasing.

The covenant was to pray for revival in Logan County until the revival came, or they died. James McGready himself, not wishing to miss the impending revival from God, moved to Logan County in the year 1796. He felt also that his work in Orange County [North Carolina] was over." [53]

Account #6:

[In Kentucky] "McGready mourned with weeping over the evil so prevalent in the community. Upon arriving at the Muddy River, Red, and Gasper River churches, he promptly set aside the third Saturday of each month for fasting and prayer, inspired by the prayer meetings of Northeastern Christians. McGready required the membership of the three churches to sign an [covenant] agreement to pray at sunset on Saturday and at sunrise on Sunday:

When we consider the word and promises of a compassionate God to the poor lost family of Adam, we find the strongest encouragement for Christians to pray in faith – to ask in the name of Jesus for the conversion of their fellow-men. None ever went to Christ when on earth, with the case of their friends, that were denied, and, although the days of his humiliation are ended, yet, for the encouragement of his people, he has left it on record, that where two or three agree upon the earth to ask in prayer, believing, it shall be done. Again, whatsoever you shall ask the Father in my name, that will I do, that the Father may be glorified in the Son. With these promises before us, we feel encouraged to unite our supplications to a prayer-hearing God for the outpouring of his Spirit, that his people may be quickened and comforted, and that our children, and sinners generally, may be converted. [54] Therefore, we bind ourselves to observe the third Saturday of each month, for one year, as a day of fasting and prayer for the conversion of sinners in Logan County, and throughout the world.

We also engage to spend one half hour every Saturday evening, beginning at the setting of the sun, and one half hour every Sabbath morning, from the rising of the sun, pleading with God to revive his work.' [55]

To this covenant, he and they affixed their names." [56]

Account #7:

From the testimony of the Reverend William Barnet, "Father McGready would so describe Heaven, that you would almost see its glories, and long to be there, and he would so array hell and its horrors before the wicked, that they would tremble and quake, imagining a lake of fire and brimstone yawning to overwhelm them, and the wrath of God thrusting them down the horrible abyss." [57]

Account #8:

"These are the sparks of revival and awakening that blazed through the frontiers of Southern Kentucky and Northern Tennessee, and then spread like wild fire from there.

The Reverend James McGready a Presbyterian minister was foremost among the early revivalists of the area. In fact, one might say that he was largely responsible for this outburst of religious fervor." [58]

Another source described him in this manner, "For subsequent years, [after the Great Revival commenced in 1800] a history of Mr. McGready would be a history of the revival. He was its leading spirit – I speak of him as a subordinate agent, of course – its most earnest advocate and powerful promoter." [59]

Account #9:

"When McGready came to Logan County [KY], he brought with him a long tradition known as the Scottish sacramental season, which was still being practiced regularly by the Presbyterian congregations.

It is clear that McGready saw a connection between the sacrament season and revival. In his written account of the events of 1800, sixteen of seventeen revival meetings were connected to sacrament observances. However, McGready also revealed his openness to innovations associated with distinctly American influences as well and actively promoted the introduction of the camp meeting into the sacrament tradition in pioneer Kentucky." [60]

Account #10:

"McGready pictured the delights of heaven and the terrors of hell in a peculiarly realistic manner." [61]

Account #11:

"In July 1800, McGready had his Pentecost–and changed the course of American history. After an initial revival at Red River, he decided to send out advance notice of the next sacramental service at Gasper River church. When word spread through the settlements scores of pioneers headed in wagons, in the saddle, and on moccasined feet for Gasper River, ready for the Spirit to work. They came from as far away as 100 miles…with tents and vittles–cold pork, slabs of corn bread, and roasted birds–ready to stay a while to see, hear, and feel the hand of God." [62]

CHAPTER 9

Leaders of the Second Great Awakening

William & John McGee, Partners in Ministry

These two brothers were united by brotherly love
and a passionate love for God.

Account #1:

"Two brothers, William and John McGee, journeyed through the Cumberland section of Kentucky and Tennessee preaching with remarkable power and the work of grace. [It] extended through those states and on into North and South Carolina, and western Virginia, and in the other direction, north of the Ohio River." [63]

Account #2:

"The first pastor of Beech [Presbyterian] Church, William McGee, was sent west from North Carolina as a missionary in the wilderness of Tennessee. He also served as pastor of Shiloh Presbyterian Church, north of Gallatin." [64]

Account #3:

"The year 1799 is distinguished for the commencement of the great revival of religion in the West and the introduction of camp meetings in the United States.

This revival commenced under the united labors of [the] two brothers, John and William McGee. The former, a Methodist local preacher, and the latter, an ordained Presbyterian minister, called to the pastoral care of a Presbyterian congregation in Sumner County, Tennessee. Both had moved with their families from North Carolina and settled near each other in Smith County [now Sumner County]. Both had received good educations preparatory for Presbyterian ministry. But, when the revolutionary struggle came on, they patriotically decided for their country to enter the army of the Whigs to battle, side by side, for liberty's cause.

Peace and the independence of the country being secured, they both returned to the private circle of their parents. Both professed conversion and the new birth under the ministry of a distinguished Methodist preacher in North Carolina, where they and their parents lived. After marriage, which occurred shortly after their return from the army, the elder, John, was made a minister of the Methodist Episcopal Church. The younger, William became a minister of the Presbyterian, according to the order respectively of those Christian denominations.

It was not long after that they, together with their families emigrated to that portion of Tennessee of which we have spoken. [It was an area that was] almost an unbroken wilderness and [they] settled on farms contiguous to each other. There they industriously engaged in the business of opening farms and cultivating the soil. William was ministering as pastor of a congregation of Presbyterians in Sumner County, while John, as a local preacher of the Methodist Church, preached in a sort of itinerant style.

[He preached] here and there, throughout that sparsely populated portion of the state, making war upon the enemies of God and man in all the potency of the word of truth.

The two brothers were ever greatly allied to each other and often attended meetings of two day's continuance in that state. In 1799, living contiguous to that part of Kentucky commonly called Green River, poorly supplied with ministers, yet rapidly filling with immigrants, to visit which they had been often urgently solicited, in the latter part of the summer, sent forth a series of appointments to hold together, two day meetings, at a number of places reaching toward the Ohio river, leaving it to the brethren contiguous to the respective places of appointment, as each meeting was to include a Sabbath, to make them sacramental meetings, or not, as might best suit their own wishes.

The first of their appointments was at Red River meetinghouse in Logan County, Ky. [It was] one of the congregations under the charge of Rev. James McGready, a Presbyterian clergyman." [65]

Account #4:

Catharine Caroline Cleveland states, "The men who promoted the revival and with whom it gained favor as the excitement increased were marked by a fervid, impressive manner of preaching. One of these, Rev. William McGee, it is related that 'he would sometimes exhort after the sermon, standing on the floor, or sitting, or lying in the dust, his eyes streaming, and his heart so full that he could only ejaculate, 'Jesus, Jesus!'" [66]

Account #5:

"Brothers William and John McGee attended one of McGready's early camp meetings and brought the revival spirit to Tennessee. John McGee, a Methodist minister, held the first known Tennessee camp meeting at Drake's Creek, Sumner County in

August 1800, and revivalism quickly spread throughout the fall of 1800 and into 1801." [67]

Account #6:

"Presbyterian William McGee was to become famous as a spirited revivalist. With his Methodist brother, John created a spiritual awakening in June 1800 at Rev. McGready's Red River, Kentucky Presbyterian revival. Both of the two visiting brothers, John and William McGee, were invited by McGready to preach." [68] "It was Methodist Episcopal preacher John McGee who, seeing that the worshippers wanted to hear more at the close of the meeting suddenly rose and paced the aisles shouting exhortations with extreme excitement. The congregation collapsed to the floor, stricken in some inexplicable way. The ministers interpreted this as a visitation of the Holy Spirit. As it was replicated in church after church in Kentucky and Tennessee, it would come to be known as evidence of a Second Great Awakening." [69]

Account #7:

"The new minister at Beech Church in 1800-01 was William McGee, a revivalist Presbyterian pastor who believed that to receive salvation, individuals should repent of their sins, ask to be saved and undergo an acute emotional experience accompanied by [the] presence of the Holy Spirit.

They would henceforth date their salvation to this euphoric feeling at a particular camp meeting or church service. It was much less important to state total allegiance to a man-made creed, such as the Westminster Confession, or to accumulate credit for good works in the community." [70]

Account #8:

"...John McGee, was a 'shouting Methodist preacher' from Middle Tennessee who went to great lengths in his sermons to arouse the feelings of the congregation to levels not attained by preachers showing greater self-restraint, genetic inhibition, or a refined sense of decorum. It is important to mention this style of John McGee's preaching, because the Second Great Awakening was heralded by extreme emotional and physical responses from worshippers during sermons." [71]

Account #9:

"Their [William and John McGee] preaching together had excited marvel in Tennessee, for their theological views had previously been thought antagonistic [Methodist and Presbyterian]. John McGee wrote that brotherly love dissolved their differences in doctrine." [72]

CHAPTER 10

Leaders of the Second Great Awakening

Barton W. Stone, Frontiersman & Evangelist

His dream was "to unite the Christians in all the sects".

Account #1:

"Another Presbyterian who attended this Logan County [KY] revival was Barton Warren Stone (1772-1844). Born in Port Tobacco, Maryland, Stone moved into western North Carolina, where he was converted under McGready. In 1800, he was serving the small Cane Ridge and Concord churches in Bourbon County, Kentucky. Greatly impressed by what he saw at Gasper River [one of McGready's churches], the more so because of his concern over the prevailing apathy in his own area, Stone adopted McGready's methods. After some preliminary revivals, he announced a great meeting to be held at Cane Ridge on August 6, 1801.

When the day arrived; so did a great many ministers, including some Baptists and Methodists, and an unbelievably large concourse of people. The crowd was estimated at from ten to twenty-five thousand – and this at a time when nearby Lexington, the state's largest city, barely exceeded two thousand. " [73]

Account #2:

Stone was the father-in-law of one of the preeminent pioneers in Tennessee, Captain William Bowen. [Bowen's house is the Bowen-Campbell House in Goodlettsville, near Mansker's Station.]

Account #3:

"Barton W. Stone, an eminent man of God and a minister of the Presbyterian Church, had charge of two congregations, Cane Ridge and Concord, in Bourbon County, KY. Religion at the time was at very low ebb in the Presbyterian Church. But in the spring of 1801, a great meeting was held near Russellville, Kentucky, and Mr. Stone, having heard of the gracious work in Tennessee and the southern portion of Kentucky, attended that meeting, at which the preachers were Messrs. McGrady [McGready], McGee, Rankin, and Hodge, of the Presbyterian Church. Mr. Stone stated that he had never before witnessed such a scene. The people were struck down powerless, and lay as though there were in the agonies of death, pleading for mercy; and after a while they would rise and tell the wonders of redeeming love. Mr. Stone soon became convinced that it was a work of God. He returned home and had a meeting the next Sabbath at Cane Ridge." [74]

Account #4:

"By 1803 the Presbyterian Church had accused two of Stone's closest colleagues of Arminianism. (Refer to Historical Terms Defined.) In 1804, Stone and six other ministers resigned from the Kentucky synod and within a year adopted the name 'Christians' and took the Bible as their only guide.

Rejecting a church hierarchy, they contended that salvation was open to all believers and that each congregation should govern its own church.

Stone spent the years from 1804 to 1832 preaching and writing in Kentucky and Tennessee. At Lexington on January 1, 1832, Stone and representatives of his own congregation and representatives of Alexander Campbell's Disciples agreed to a form of unity that became the Disciples of Christ." [75]

Account #5:

John Carr gives this personal insight on Stone, "I have always viewed Barton W. Stone as a great and good man. He was a man of remarkable humility and modesty. These traits of his character were known wherever he was known. He was a man of peace; and it was a pity, I think, that he, with his party in Kentucky, did not make the same stand that the Cumberland Presbyterians made in this country. If they had stricken out [eliminated] the doctrine of unconditional election and reprobation from the Confession of Faith, or formed a new creed and discipline, and called themselves the Kentucky Presbyterians, I think their course would have contributed to the advancement of the gospel. But doubtless Mr. Stone did what he thought was best in the case. He was a great instrument in the revival of 1800 in Kentucky. He travelled and preached nearly to his last days. He died in 1844, in Hannibal, Missouri at the house of his son-in-law, Capt. William Bowen; and I am told he gave ample and cheering testimony of his entrance upon a bright and glorious immortality beyond the valley and shadow of death. I knew Barton W. Stone, and I would do injustice to myself if I were not to say that I viewed him as a great and good man." [76]

CHAPTER 11

Leaders of the Second Great Awakening

Francis Asbury, Father of American Methodism

"Give me one hundred preachers who fear nothing but sin and desire nothing but God…" John Wesley

Account #1:

"Born in 1745 near Birmingham, England, Asbury succumbed early to the religiosity of his mother and found his inspiration in John Wesley and other leaders of Methodism. After his conversion, he labored diligently during the 1760's as an itinerant preacher in the Midlands." [77]

Account #2:

"Frances Asbury (1745-1816) was America's greatest Methodist leader…he became a Christian by 1759. After working as a blacksmith from 1759 to 1765, he became a local preacher about 1766. After serving on several circuits during the period from 1766 to 1771, he came to America in 1771 at his own request. He became [John] Wesley's general assistant in America. He preached all through the middle and southern colonies. He set up a system of circuit riders to spread Methodism swiftly and widely…

…Asbury traveled 300,000 miles, preached tirelessly, and received several thousand preachers into the American Methodist Church…

The Methodists in America numbered over 200,000 by the time of Asbury's death. He did this work even though he was often ill with many ailments." [78]

Account #3:

"When Wesley announced in 1771 that their American brothers needed help, Asbury did not hesitate to embark for the New World (and started, at Wesley's urging, the journal that would become a basic sourcebook of church history). Arriving in Philadelphia that October, he quickly set about forming new preaching circuits, traveling widely, and organizing the ragtag forces of Methodism. By not deserting his flock during the Revolution (despite Wesley's advice), and by the right combination of steel and compromise, he eventually emerged as the leader of American Methodism." [79]

Account #4:

"Gradually, the Methodists and ministers of other faiths made progress in their war against Satan, culminating in the Second Great Awakening around the turn of the century (1800). It was a time of fervent revivalism, recommitment to God, heavy doses of hell-fire and damnation preaching, and the harvesting of souls. James McGready, a Presbyterian, is generally credited with initiating a type of revivalism that would continue for a generation – the camp meeting, where people would gather from miles around and spend anywhere from one night to a week. The Methodist penchant for organization, however, quickly enabled Asbury and his associates to bring the camp meeting to its most effective form.

Such gatherings were especially important on the frontier, for they offered both spiritual sustenance and an opportunity to leaven a hardscrabble existence with social intercourse.

Asbury often witnessed several thousand people at these meetings; one of the most spectacular, at Cane Ridge, Kentucky, in the summer of 1801, attracted a crowd of more than twenty thousand." [80]

Account #5:

"The life of a Methodist circuit rider was not an easy one. We may characterize this life with Bishop Asbury's own experiences because he kept a journal and traveled incessantly. He set an example of rugged perseverance for his men to emulate... He rode nearly 300,000 miles, presided at 224 annual conferences and ordained about 4,000 preachers.

Here is an Asbury diary entry from May 11, 1790. 'Crossed Kentucky River. Our way is over mountains, steep hills, deep rivers, and muddy creeks; a thick growth of reeds for miles together; and no inhabitants but wild beasts and savage men... we ate no regular meal; our bread grew short, and I was much spent'" (Filson 335). "[81]

Account #6:

Having known Asbury well, John Carr states, "I believe it was in 1815, I saw Bishop Asbury for the last time... The old soldier of the cross was then nearly worn out in the conflicts of life, and he appeared to me the most venerable man on whom I had ever rested my eyes.

The hair of his head was perfectly white, and his natural strength had so far abated, he had to be lifted from his horse and helped into the stand erected for preaching the funeral of Bishop Coke, who had some time before died at sea. The text was Acts 11:24: For he 'was a good man, and full of the Holy Ghost, and of faith'; and much people was added unto the Lord. Bishop Coke, it is known, had ordained Bishop Asbury in England. Though advanced in life and feeble in health, Bishop Asbury spoke so as to be plainly understood by an immense concourse of people, and the effect of his preaching was very remarkable. The most solemn awe seemed to fill every heart and shaded every face. Really, I thought if the enemy of souls had been present in person, he would have been compelled to behave himself by reason of the impressiveness of the exercises that day. Upon the adjournment of the Conference, Bishop Asbury turned his course towards the North, with the hope of meeting the ensuring General Conference, to be held the next May in Baltimore. But he died, I learned, before reaching his journey's end, March 31, 1816; thus, passed away from us, a great and good man." [82]

Account #7:

"Dr. Salter says this of Asbury. '...the bishop never asked anyone to go where he himself was unwilling to go, and in all likelihood had not already been.' May God rekindle such leadership among us again." [83]

CHAPTER 12

 Leaders of the Second Great Awakening

Methodist Circuit Riders, Mighty Men of God

"I know not from whence they all come,
unless from the clouds." [84]

Account #1:

"In the early days of the American Methodist Church, there weren't enough pastors to go around. So, the church instituted circuit riders–pastors who rode from one town to the next, on a planned route [circuit] that sometimes took 5-6 weeks." [85]

Account #2:

"Methodists gained the most in the South thanks to [Devereux] Jarratt's revival preaching, which brought thousands into the church, and to Asbury's circuit riders, lay preachers, and class meetings. The diligence of the Methodist circuit riders was attested to by the common saying about foul weather: 'There is nothing out today but crows and Methodist preachers.'" [86]

Account #3:

"From this vast scope of country the preachers came [Mississippi Valley Annual Conference] and met together, [Methodist Episcopal Conference] like a band of brothers. They were, indeed, itinerants of the old Wesleyan stamp. They were plain men in dress, their coats all being cut in the same style, their manners generally showing that they were not in the least degree inclined to the indulgence of superfluities of any kind.

None of them, I will add, wore the D.D. [Doctor of Divinity] attached to their names for distinction's sake; but brothers in love, as such, simply then addressed each other. " [87]

'They conveyed a stern visage, these young preachers. When they entered a space where teenagers were dancing, their disapproval was palpable.'

[Barton Stone gave the following description] He said, 'About this time came in a few Methodist preachers. Their appearance was prepossessing, grave, holy, meek, plain and humble. Their very presence checked all levity in all around them; their zeal was fervent and unaffected, and their preaching was often electric on the congregation, and fixed their attention.'" [88]

Account #4:

This early frontier ministry was often lonely and dangerous. Samuel Wakefield wrote a hymn about the perils circuit riders faced. It describes the circuit rider's family anxiously waiting for his return, and the final stanza says:

> "Yet still they look with glistening eye,
> Till lo! a herald hastens nigh;
> He comes the tale of woe to tell,
> How he, their prop and glory fell;
> How died he in a stranger's room,
> How strangers laid him in the tomb,
> How spoke he with his latest breath,
> And loved and blessed them all in death." [89]

Account #5:

"While it was the camp meetings that provided a venue to present the gospel and gather a harvest time of souls from the scattered westerners, it was the circuit riding Methodist preachers, who called on their isolated homes and taught them how to be disciples of Christ. These itinerant laymen were the backbone of the successful growth of the Methodist Church in the first half of the 19th Century.

The Methodist organization was a well-conceived network that was designed to reach every person on the frontier. The circuit rider traveled a range of 200 to 500 miles. He stopped at 'classes' or 'stations' for preaching appointments in homes, under trees, and in taverns. Each location had a class leader and 10-20 people in the 'congregation.'

He usually made his rounds about every 4-5 weeks. These mobile ministers prepared their sermons on horseback and preached almost every day and sometimes twice: morning and evening. No area was too remote to be outside the reach of the Methodist system.

The circuit preacher was usually single, and had little more than a common school education. In 1800 there were no Methodist seminaries. He did not give his sermons from erudite notes, but used homespun stories to apply the biblical offer of free-grace to all. For his grueling schedule he received $80 a year in1800.

The Methodist organization was peerless in the Protestant church. The circuit rider was appointed by the presiding elder, who was the district superintendent.

The traveling itinerant was shifted to another circuit every year or two by order of the Methodist manual called the Discipline. Each district was assigned to a regional unit called the Conference, and every four years a 'Quadrennial Conference' was held. At the top of the structure was the bishop, and Francis Asbury was the most famous and the most powerful, too." [90]

Account #6:

"It was the circuit riding preachers of the Methodist church who helped to spread much of the revival fire. Circuit riders often traversed dangerous venues in order to bring the gospel to the frontier. One-half of these brave soldiers of the cross died before their thirty-third birthday." [91]

These men gave up reputations, even the basics of comfort, and literally sacrificed their lives (as most did not live past middle age due to the grueling nature of their mission) to become bearers of eternal light and life to those living in darkness. Their names, and much of what was accomplished for the Kingdom of God through them, are recorded only in Heaven.

"The noise was like the roar of Niagara.
The vast sea of human beings seemed to be agitated
as if by a storm…
Some of the people were singing, others praying,
some crying for mercy.
A peculiarly strange sensation came over me.
My heart beat tumultuously; my knees trembled, my lips quivered,
and I felt as though I must fall to the ground…
The scene was…indescribable. "

An eyewitness account of a camp meeting.

CHAPTER 13

 Characteristics of a Camp Meeting

This section is to give the readers a taste of what many sacramental meetings had in common, according to the insights of a diverse collection of voices.

"Camp Meeting of the Methodists in N. America", 1819, Library of Congress

Account #1:

"The camps were arranged in a circle, rectangle, or horseshoe with a brush fence having two gates. Plank seats were set before covered raised platforms for preachers. A pen for 'seekers' was set off by rails in front. Boys called 'runners' chased out the hogs and dogs. Sermons, delivered at 11 A.M., 3:00 P.M. and 7:00 P.M., were preceded by the singing of simple folk hymns – some of them doggerel – with an oft-repeated refrain. There was a prayer meeting at 7:00 A.M. People brought their own food and slept in wagons or on the ground.

The camp meeting was accompanied by emotional and physical phenomena, such as 'falling', 'rolling', 'jerks', (of the head from side to side or back and forth), 'barking' on all fours (like dogs), dancing, singing, or laughing. In discussing these physical phenomena, one should remember that these people lived in isolated cabins, often in danger from Indians, and in close touch with nature.

Their religious experience, compressed into the few days of the camp meeting, often became intense. The wonder is that there was so little emotion, and the preachers did oppose excess emotionalism." [92]

Account #2:

"One observer describes a typical camp meeting this way:

'The glare of the blazing camp-fires falling on a dense assemblage of heads simultaneously bowed in adoration and reflected back from long ranges of tents upon every side; hundreds of candles and lamps suspended among the trees, together with numerous torches flashing to and fro, throwing an uncertain light upon the tremulous foliage, and giving an appearance of dim and indefinite extent to the depth of the forest; the solemn chanting of hymns swelling and falling on the night wind; the impassioned exhortations; the earnest prayers; the sobs, shrieks, or shouts, bursting from persons under intense agitation of mind; the sudden spasms which seized upon scores, and unexpectedly dashed them to the ground – all conspired to invest the scene with terrific interest and to work up the feelings to the highest pitch of excitement.

When we add to this, the lateness of the hour to which the exercises were protracted, sometimes till two in the morning, or longer; the eagerness of curiosity stimulated for so long a time previous; the reverent enthusiasm which ascribed the strange contortions witnessed, to the mysterious agency of God; the fervent and sanguine temperament of some of the preachers; and lastly, the boiling zeal of the Methodists, who could not refrain from shouting aloud during the sermon, and shaking hands all round afterwards.'" [93]

Account #3:

"Camp meetings were rural by nature. Scheduled so as not to interfere with the farming cycle, they were usually held within an outcropping of trees near a stream or other body of fresh water. Transportation was slow and primitive, so any meeting more than a few miles from home required that attendees stay overnight. Individuals and families planned provisions for several days and 'camped' for the length of the revival. Public orators were the celebrities of the day, and attending public speaking events was a favorite form of entertainment for rural folk who normally had infrequent outside contact during their daily routines. Camp meetings were festive, on a par with the excitement generated by county fairs and political campaigns. Poverty and isolation were common in rural Appalachia, and camp meetings provided rare opportunities for folks to get away from their hard existence and visit with friends and neighbors." [94]

Account #4:

"All the blessed displays of Almighty power and grace, all the sweet gales of the divine Spirit, and soul-reviving showers of the blessings of Heaven which we enjoyed before, and which we considered wonderful beyond conception; were but like a few scattering drops before a mighty rain, when compared with the overflowing floods of salvation, which the eternal, gracious Jehovah has poured out like a mighty river, upon this our guilty, unworthy country. The Lord has indeed shewed [showed] himself a prayer-hearing God: he has given his people a praying spirit and a lively faith, and then he has answered their prayers far beyond their highest expectations." [95]

Account #5:

"At a typical Communion, Saturday was mostly devoted to fasting and small-group prayer as people solemnly prepared themselves for Sunday's Communion." [96]

Account #6:

"Barton Stone devoted a whole chapter of his memoirs to a description of the outward manifestations of strong religious emotions [which were] …not only a landmark in the history of revivalism, but a cause of controversy and schism.

'The bodily agitations or exercises, attending the excitement in the beginning of this century, were various, and called by various names. …The *falling* exercise was very common among all classes, the saints and sinners of every age and of every grade, from the philosopher to the clown.

The subject of this exercise would, generally, with a piercing scream, fall like a log on the floor, earth, or mud, and appear as dead…

The *jerks* cannot be so easily described. Sometimes the subject of the jerks would be affected in some one member of the body, and sometimes the whole system. When the head alone was affected, it would be jerked backward and forward, or from side to side, so quickly that the features of the face could not be distinguished. When the whole system was affected, I have seen the person stand in one place, and jerk backward and forward in quick succession, their head nearly touching the floor behind and before. All classes, saints and sinners, the strong as well as the weak, were thus affected…

The *dancing* exercise: This generally began with the jerks, and was peculiar to the professors of religion. The subject, after jerking awhile, began to dance, and then the jerks would cease. Such dancing was indeed heavenly to the spectators; there was nothing in it like levity, nor calculated to excite levity in the beholders. The smile of heaven shone on the countenance of the subject, and assimilated to angels appeared the whole person. Sometimes the motion was quick and sometimes slow. Thus they continued to move forward and backward in the same track or alley until nature seemed exhausted, and they would fall prostrate on the floor or earth, unless caught by those standing by. While thus exercised, I have heard their solemn praises and prayers ascending to God.

The *barking* exercise, (as opposers contemptuously called it) was nothing but the jerks. A person affected with the jerks, especially in his head, would often make a grunt, or bark, if you please, from the suddenness of the jerk...

The *laughing* exercise was frequent, confined solely with the religious. It was loud, hearty laughter, but *sui generis* [Latin phrase, meaning of its own kind; in a class by itself; unique]; it excited laughter in none else. The subject appeared rapturously solemn, and his laughter excited solemnity in saints and sinners. It is truly indescribable.

The *running* exercise was nothing more than, that persons feeling something of these bodily agitations, through fear, attempted to run away, and thus escape from them; but it commonly happened that they ran not far, before they fell, or became so greatly agitated that they could proceed no farther...

I shall close this chapter with the *singing* exercise. This is more unaccountable than anything else I ever saw. The subject in a very happy state of mind would sing most melodiously, not from the mouth or nose, but entirely in the breast, the sounds issuing from thence. Such music silenced everything, and attracted the attention of all. It was most heavenly; none could ever tire of hearing it.'" [97]

Account #7:

"The focus of the sacrament season was participation in The Lord's Supper. For Scots-Irish Presbyterians, inclusion in this ritual was guarded closely and accompanied by several symbols of exclusivity. First, preparation was necessary on the part of the communicant as well as the ministers charged with interviewing each person in advance and approving his sincerity and worthiness. Communion tokens, small emblems made usually from lead and stamped with the date, and sometimes the initials of the minister, were required for admission to communion.

Once admitted to the table, the exclusivity ended as all participants – male and female, young and old, cleric and lay person, served one another common bread and wine representing the body and blood of Christ." [98]

Account #8:

"Our love-feasts were conducted differently from what they are now. An early custom was, they came into love-feasts by tickets; and if tickets were not distributed, a prudent, pious man was placed at the door, and no one was admitted into love-feast who wore ruffles, or rings, or jewelry of any description.

They were politely told by the door-keeper that they could not have entrance there with those ornaments on. I would just observe at this period of my narrative, if this rule were observed as it was in early times, but few, and very few, of our female friends would enter the house of God to partake of love-feast. We scarcely ever failed, under these circumstances, of having a glorious feast." [99]

Author's Note: I am including the following two accounts to show the way an individual, Thomas Cleland, viewed a camp meeting that impacted him forcefully as he had experienced it [Account #9], and then his view of it in retrospect years later after receiving an education in theology which altered his perspective on what he had experienced [Account #10].

Account #9:

"As a young and diligent Presbyterian pilgrim in Kentucky around 1800, Thomas Cleland regularly attended sacramental occasions. At the Cane Ridge sacrament in 1801, Cleland was particularly caught up in the power of the occasion. Enthralled by an action sermon on a familiar text from the Song of Songs – 'Rise up my love, my fair one, and come away' – he was suddenly overwhelmed. 'My heart was melted! My bosom heaved! My eyes, for the first time, were a fountain of tears.' This 'weeping, dissolved, humbled situation' lasted, Cleland said, through the rest of the sermon and through 'seven courses of [the] sacramental service.' This powerful experience at the Cane Ridge Communion marked a high point in Cleland's spiritual life." [100]

Account #10:

"A little more than two decades after this Communion [Cane Ridge meeting described above], Cleland – unlettered layman turned cleric – began dismantling within his church the Eucharistic rituals in which he had earlier participated with such fervor. The long tables and old benches were removed; communicants were now to remain in their pews and receive the elements there. Tokens too were 'dispensed with' and the rituals that went with them – for the sake of 'convenience.' The 'old plan' for the Communions was unwieldy and inefficient; it simply consumed too much time. Streamlined quarterly Communions replaced the annual festivities of the summer and early fall gatherings.

Cleland, having become a doctor of divinity, was in retrospect almost embarrassed by his earlier devotional zeal during the Communion seasons – particularly by his weeping response at Cane Ridge and by his 'extravagant notions' about the power of the sacramental elements and the dangers of an unworthy approach.

All this, he suggested, was evidence of his erstwhile ignorance and 'want of religious training.' The difference between Cleland's youthful devotion in the 1790s and his calm revisions of worship in the 1820s suggests in miniature the fate of the sacramental season." [101]

These are images of actual metal tokens
that would have been used for sacramental meetings
in the 1700's and 1800's.

Communion tokens from 1765, 1776, 1788 and 1833.

"Let us love our God supremely,
let us love each other too;
let us love and pray for sinners,
till our God makes all things new.
Then He'll call us home to heaven,
at His table we'll sit down.
Christ will gird Himself and serve us
with sweet manna all around."

From the song, *Brethren, We Have Met Together*
written by George Atkins in 1819.

CHAPTER 14

Locations of the Second Great Awakening

Red River Church in Logan County, Kentucky

Rev. James McGready, Pastor

Account #1: **First Perspective** on the meeting in 1799.

[After moving to Logan County, Kentucky and taking responsibility for three infant congregations] "McGready worked hard, preaching and praying during these two years with steady results, but nothing spectacular happened until the power of God manifested itself at a service in the Red River Church and the Gasper River Church in July of 1799. When revival broke out, dozens of members in the congregations were '*slain in the spirit*' as the Holy Spirit moved in the services. When the news spread around the countryside, anticipation for what might happen at the next meeting stirred the curiosity of everyone and interest soared. But, a cold winter caused larger meetings to be postponed in the overflowing churches. In June of 1800, several hundred devout Christians met for a Communion service at the Red River Meetinghouse. The congregation was composed of McGready's three churches. McGready was assisted by four other men: John Rankin and Reverend William Hodge, also two brothers named John and William McGee." [102]

Account #2: **Second Perspective** on the meeting in 1799.

..."on the last Sunday of July 1799, at a Communion meeting at the Red River church, members again seriously responded to their minister's exhortations. Monday evening most of the congregation lingered around the door after the service, as if unwilling to leave without having their hopes fulfilled. After a brief consultation, McGready and the assisting ministers agreed to call the people back into the church, and then the preachers delivered long, passionate prayers and admonitions. Under these intense urgings, many members of the congregation felt themselves enlivened in spirit, comforted, and convicted. Their zeal increased their striving for repentance and God's forgiveness and mercy.

'About this time,' as recorded by McGready. 'a remarkable spirit of prayer and supplication was given to Christians, and a sensible, heart-felt burden of the dreadful state of sinners out of Christ: so that it might be said with propriety, that Zion travailed in birth to bring forth her spiritual children.'" [103]

Account #3:

"As renewal gently rippled from the seaboard to the Appalachians, a rousing, roaring revival shook the West. It started in the most unlikely place: Logan County in the southwestern corner of Kentucky and more notoriously known as *Rogues' Harbor.'*

The most unsavory characters had covenanted with one another to keep out law and order, and any 'regulators' who would steal their lawbreaking freedoms. They were refugees from every known crime." [104]

<u>Account #4:</u> **First Perspective** on meeting in 1800.

"The first of their [William and John McGee] appointments was [1800] at Red River meeting-house, in Logan County, Ky., one of the congregations under the charge of Rev. James McGready, a Presbyterian clergyman. It was announced as a sacramental occasion. The two brothers McGee came duly to their appointment, and were met by the Rev. Wm. Hodge, John Rankin, and James McGready. On Saturday the pulpit was filled by William McGee, who delivered an interesting discourse, well adapted to a preparation of the congregation to participate in the Eucharistic [at the] last of the next day. The assembling of the people was reasonably numerous. The order of the next day's services was, a sermon in the forenoon by Rev. Mr. Hodge, to be followed by a sermon from Rev. John McGee, and accordingly they took their positions in the pulpit.

A large congregation for that sparsely peopled neighborhood gathered and filled the large old log house very well. Mr. Hodge arose and as he was often heard afterwards addressed the assembly with a freedom and power of speech he had never felt before. Still, however, the hearers though riveted in their attention, remained silent and quiet.

As he closed his discourse, the Rev. John McGee arose singing,

'Come Holy Spirit, heavenly dove,

with all Thy quick'ning powers,

Kindle a flame of sacred love in these cold hearts of ours.'"

He had not more than sang through the verse quoted, ere an aged lady, Mrs. Racely, sitting quite across the congregation, to his left, and Mrs. Clark, also advanced in years, somewhat to his right, began in rather suppressed, yet distinct tones of voice to hold a sort of dialogue with each other, and to reciprocate sentiments of praise and gladness to the 'Most High,' for His grace and goodness in redemption. Still the preacher sang on — still the venerable ladies in louder terms praised God! The preacher, yet singing this beautiful and most supplicatory hymn, came down from the pulpit intending to take the hands of those two happy sisters, shaking hands as he passed, with all those within his reach. Instantly they fell as he progressed through the crowd — some as dead men and women — some most piteously crying for mercy, and a few, here and there, lifting their voices high in the praise of the Redeemer. Among these last was the Rev. Wm. McGee, who fell to the floor, and, though shouting praises, was for some time so overpowered with the divine [unreadable word] that he was not able to rise. The other ministers, McGready, Hodge, and Rankin, were so surprised and astonished with this apparent confusion, in the house of the Lord that they made their way to and out at the door, and there continued for some minutes, whisperingly inquiring of one another, 'What is to be done?' There they might have remained yet longer, had not Mr. Hodge, who returned to the door, and seeing all on the floor, praying or praising, said to his reverend brethren :

'We can do nothing. If this be of Satan, it will soon come to an end. But if of God, our efforts and fears are vain! I think it is of God, and [we will] join in giving glory to His name.'

He walked into the house, while the others presently followed. Rapidly some of those who fell to the floor, mourning and crying for mercy, rose, sometimes two or more at the same moment, shouting praise for the evidences they felt in their souls of sins forgiven — for 'redeeming grace, and dying love!' So there remained no more place, that day, for preaching, or the administering of the sacrament. From thirty to forty that evening professed conversion, and to have found 'peace with God, through our Lord, Jesus Christ.'" [105]

Account #5: **Second Perspective** on the meeting in 1800.

"When the revival began, it began without warning. At a meeting at Red River Meetinghouse in June of 1800, though some attendees cried and wept, and others fell to the floor under conviction of their sinfulness, and though there were conversions, it seemed, as the last day of the meetings closed, that there would be no great move of God at that time. Disappointed, James McGready and two ministers who had been assisting him left the building.

A visiting minister from nearby Sumner County, Tennessee, William McGee, looking sorrowfully around, suddenly felt impressed to shout to the people, 'Let the Lord God Omnipotent reign in your hearts!' At this, pandemonium broke forth among the congregation. Some of the lost began to scream, others fell to the floor, sometimes writhing, sometimes perfectly still, having swooned, as fainting was called in that day. In modern religious terminology, they had been 'slain in the spirit'. (Describing the event years later, McGee said that he felt as if one greater than himself was speaking.) Several members went to McGee and urged him to try to stop what was happening, saying that

Presbyterians (this was a Presbyterian congregation) could not allow such goings on. Instead, William McGee went throughout the building, shouting praises to God and encouraging the people to yield themselves wholly to God. Many were changed forever that night. In the words of James McGready, *'a mighty effusion of* [God's] *Spirit'* came upon the people, 'and the floor was soon covered with the slain; their screams for mercy pierced the heavens.'" [106]

Account #6: **A Third Perspective** on the meeting in 1800.*****

"In June 1800, at the Annual Red River Communion, more than five hundred people gathered from McGready's three congregations. Many traveled from as far away as sixty miles to attend. Because there were too many people for one man to serve, McGready secured five area pastors to help him administer Communion and preach the Word. They included two brothers, John and William McGee, a Methodist and a Presbyterian respectively. Their sermons were simple and plainspoken, dealing with hell, heaven, and salvation for all who would believe. The meeting grew so large that they elected to move it outdoors. For three days, matters were orderly, serious, fervent, solemn, and sincere. Then a tangible sense of God's presence swept the congregation." [107] John McGee felt an irresistible urge to preach, and the people were eager to hear him. He began, and scores were converted.

Author's Note: I have included multiple separate accounts of the same meeting at Red River in 1799 and 1800 because each contains additional details that may provide helpful insight to the reader. Some repetition will be noted in these accounts.

Account #7:

"On the third Sabbath of June, a sacramental meeting, attended by their three congregations, was held at the Red River Meetinghouse. McGready, the minister of the congregation, speaks of it in glowing terms:

'This was indeed a blessed day of the Son of Man--The Lord afforded more than common light, life and zeal to his ministers, and more than common life to the exercise of his praying people. Upon every day of the occasion, there were visible tokens of the love and goodness of God. Christians were filled with joy and peace in believing; and poor distressed, condemned sinners were brought to see the glory and fullness of a crucified Jesus, and to feel the power and efficacy of his merits and atonement. . . . We have reason to believe that the number truly and savingly brought to Christ, on this occasion, and till the Tuesday night following, was about ten persons.'

Rankin, who was an assisting minister, has this to say about the meeting:

'But wonderful to be seen and heard; on a sudden, an alarming cry burst from the midst of the deepest silence; some were thrown into wonderful and strange contortions of features, body and limbs, frightful to the beholder--others had singular gestures, with words and actions quite inconsistent with Presbyterian order and usage--all was alarm and confusion for the moment. . . . When this alarming occurrence subsided in outward show, the united congregations returned to their respective abodes, in contemplation of what they had seen, heard and felt on this most impressive occasion.'" [108]

CHAPTER 15

 Locations of the Second Great Awakening

Beech Meetinghouse in Sumner County, Tennessee

Rev. William McGee, Pastor

For purposes of clarification, Beech Meetinghouse [on Long Hollow Pike] was located close to a branch of Drake's Creek, but it is not to be confused with Drake's Creek Meetinghouse which was located on land donated by James Sanders near what is now Sanders Ferry Park in Hendersonville.

Account #1:

"This was the next meeting that was held on Saturday and Sunday following the meeting at the Red River Meetinghouse in Logan County, KY.

The location of this meeting was ten miles west of Gallatin, Sumner County; where was present a vast assembly and where were witnessed scenes similar to those described at the Red River Meetinghouse." [109]

Account #2:

"Rev. Hugh Kirkpatrick of the Beech Church left an account of one camp meeting on the site of the Beech Church in which there were 500 conversions and 125 additions to the Beech Church. Those who attended camped in a grove of beech trees which stood in front of the present [day] stone building." [110]

Account #3:

"Their next appointment was for the Saturday and Sabbath following, at what is to this day called the Beech meeting-house, situated a little south-east of the Cumberland Ridge, ten miles west of Gallatin, Sumner County, Tennessee, and seventeen miles north-east of Nashville. Hither, even on Saturday, many hundreds of the inhabitants of the adjacent country, in earnest and anxious haste, from a considerable distance around, had come. The news of the wonderful power displayed, at the Red River meeting, on the Sabbath preceding, and 'the time of refreshing from the presence of the Lord,' poured out on that occasion, had spread, as if by electric communication, together with the announcement of the preaching by the brothers at the Beech Meetinghouse, throughout much of the Green River portion of Kentucky and of all Middle Tennessee. Some came to witness and catch, if happily they might, 'these touches of His love,' some to pray and praise, while a far greater number came to witness, analyze and expose what they were pleased to stigmatize with the stereotyped phrases and brands of infidelity in every land, and country, and in all ages, 'fanaticism wild-fire and hypocrisy.'

At 11 o'clock, A. M., the two brothers, John and William McGee, were at their posts, met by other ministers of the Presbyterian and Methodist orders, to learn and know for themselves what this strange matter meant. The preaching commenced.

The Rev. John McGee commenced the services; and the writer of these narratives well remembers to have heard from the lips of that venerable old man, when speaking of the events of that time, and of the occurrences, particularly, at Beech meeting-house, when at a camp meeting near the same place, in Sumner County, about thirty years after. He quoted the words from Acts 11, verse 15, heading this chapter. 'And as I began to speak, the Holy Ghost fell on them, as on us in the beginning.' And said, 'hundreds fell and began to rejoice, or plead for pardoning mercy. Too many, very many, it proved a most joyous season and little less than one hundred of the gathered crowds of sinners professed peace through faith in Christ.'" [111]

Account #4:

"The 'camp meeting' was a unique part of the great revival which swept across the American frontier of 1800. The camp meetings at Beech were held on the land which William Montgomery and Francis Ketring sold to Trustees, John McMurtry and James Kirkpatrick, for fifty cents... The people came from distant communities and camped in the grove of Beech trees that stood immediately in front of the present building. Methodists and Presbyterians both worshiped in the old log church situated on the campground. Bishop Francis Asbury may have preached here, for the Bishop's journal has an entry on October 21, 1800, which gives an account of attending a camp meeting on Drake's Creek.*

He says, 'Yesterday and especially during the night, were witnessed scenes of deep interest. In the intervals between preaching, the people refreshed themselves and horses, and returned upon the ground. The stand was in the open air, embosomed in the wood of lofty Beech trees.

The ministers of God, Methodists and Presbyterians, united their labors and mingled with the childlike simplicity of primitive times. We suppose there were at least 30 souls converted at that meeting.'" [112]

CHAPTER 16

Locations of the Second Great Awakening

Gasper River Church in Logan County, Kentucky

Rev. James McGready, Pastor

Account #1:

"Thus it was at The Lord's Supper at Gasper River on the fourth Sabbath of July, 1798, that the flame of revival broke forth. Of this meeting, McGready records:

'This was indeed a very solemn time throughout; but especially on Monday, the Lord poured out his Spirit in a very remarkable manner, to the awakening of a great number of persons; very few families could be found in the congregation, where less or more were not deeply and solemnly impressed.'" [113]

Account #2:

According to our sources in the previous Red River section, it is clear that there was a meeting at Gasper River church soon after the initial meeting at Red River in July of 1799.

Account #3:

[The following account was written by Reverend John Rankin, who was asked to take the oversight of the Gasper River congregation by Rev. McGready, due to his traveling schedule]:

"In August, 1799 [fourth Sabbath], a sacrament was appointed at Gasper River, old meetinghouse five miles below South Union. The preachers attended, gifts were given to men, their [our] language was clothed with power which pervaded the congregation, many were convicted, some called on their neighbors to pray for them, & one under a view of his exposure to Justice, asked in consternation of soul: 'Is there no hand to stay the Justice of God?' some few could rejoice in hopes of mercy & promise of God, et cetera." [114]

Account #4:

"At Gasper River, on the fourth Sabbath of June [1800], a surprising multitude of people collected, many from a very great distance, even from the distance of thirty to sixty, and one hundred miles. On Friday and Saturday there was a very solemn attention. On Saturday evening, after the congregation was dismissed, as a few serious, exercised Christians were sitting conversing together, and appeared to be more than commonly engaged, the flame started from them and overspread the whole house until every person appeared less or more engaged. [Among] the greater part of the multitude there could be found some awakened souls struggling in the pangs of the new birth, ready to faint and die for Christ, almost upon the brink of desperation. Others again were just lifted from the horrible pit, and beginning to lisp the first notes of the new song, and to tell the sweet wonders which they saw in Christ. Ministers and experienced Christians were everywhere engaged in praying, exhorting, conversing and trying to lead inquiring souls to the Lord Jesus. In this exercise the night was spent until near the break of day.

The Sabbath was a blessed day in every sense of the word. The groans of awakened sinners could be heard all over the house during the morning sermon, but by no means so as to disturb the assembly. It was a comfortable time with many at the [Communion] table. Mr. McGee preached in the evening upon the account of Peter's sinking in the waves. In the application of his sermon the power of God seemed to shake the whole assembly. Toward the close of the sermon the cries of the distressed arose almost as loud as his voice. After the congregation was dismissed the solemnity increased till the greater part of the multitude seemed engaged in the most solemn manner. No person appeared to wish to go home; hunger and sleep seemed to affect nobody. Eternal things were the vast concern. Here awakening and converting work was to be found in every part of the multitude and even some things strangely and wonderfully new to me [James McGready].

Sober professors [those who professed to be Christians], who had been communicants [those who participated in Communion] for many years, now lying prostrate on the ground, crying out in such language as this: 'I have been a sober professor, I have been a communicant; O, I have been deceived, I have no religion.' The greater part of the multitude continued at the meeting-house all night, and no person appeared uneasy for food or sleep.

On Monday, a vast concourse of people came together. This was another day of the Son of Man. With propriety, we could adopt the language of this patriarch, and say, 'The Lord is here: how dreadful is this place! It is none other but the house of God and the very gate of heaven!' Two powerful sermons were preached by Messrs. McGee and Hodge. The almighty power of God attended the word to the hearts of many, and a universal solemnity overspread the whole assembly. When the congregation was dismissed, no person seemed to wish to leave the place. The solemnity increased, and conviction seemed to spread from heart to heart. Little children, young men and women, and old gray-headed people, persons of every description, white and black, were to be found in every part of the multitude, pricked to the heart with clear, rational, scriptural convictions, crying out for mercy in the most extreme distress; whilst every now and then we could find one and another delivered from their burden of sin and guilt by sweet believing views of the glory of God in the face of Jesus Christ. In such exercises the multitude continued at the meetinghouse till Tuesday morning after sunrise, when they broke up after they were dismissed by prayer, and indeed the circumstance of their parting added to the solemnity of the occasions. The number that, we hope were savingly brought to Christ on this occasion were forty-five persons." [115]

Account #5:

"There was a sacramental meeting at Red River in July of which McGready writes in glowing terms. This was followed by a sacramental meeting at Gasper River on the fourth Sabbath of August. Rankin tells us:

'After the congregation was dismissed, the principal subjects of the operation, sat fettered to the ground, with their heads bowed down: They trembled & shook in silence, & frequently burst into tears of sorrow for their loss. I felt refreshed in spirit & thankful to God in the ministration of the spirit of light, hope & promise to my guilty & depraved fellow man.'" [116]

Account #6:

[Of that same meeting the John Rankin described above, McGready gave this colorful description]:

"The Almighty power of God at this time was displayed in the most striking manner. On Monday, a general solemnity seized the greater part of the multitude; many persons were so struck with deep, heart-piercing convictions, that their bodily strength was quite overcome, so that they fell on the ground, and could not refrain from bitter groans and outcries for mercy. The work was general with old and young, white and black. . . . In other places, many poor, giddy persons, who, on the first days of the solemnity, could not behave with common decency, now lying prostrate on the ground, weeping, praying and crying for mercy. But time would fail to record every particular. In a word, it was day of general awakening; several person on that day, we hope, were savingly brought to Christ; and in the space of three weeks after, above twenty of those awakened gave the most clear, satisfying accounts of their views of the glory and fullness of the Mediator, and the sweet application of his blood and merits to their souls." [117]

Account #7:

"Convinced that God was moving, McGready and his colleagues planned another camp meeting to be held in late July 1800 at Gasper River. They had not anticipated what occurred. An enormous crowd—as many as 8,000—began arriving at the appointed date, many from distances as great as 100 miles. Tents were set up everywhere, wagons with provisions brought in, trees felled and their logs cut to be used as seats.

Although the term camp meeting was not used until 1802, this was the first true camp meeting where a continuous outdoor service was combined with camping out.

After three tense days, the emotions of these backwoods people used to loneliness were at the boiling point. At a huge evening meeting lighted by flaming torches, a Presbyterian pastor named William McGee gave a throbbing message on a doubting Peter sinking beneath the waves. McGready recalled:

'The Gasper River camp meeting was the turning point of the Awakening in the West. Interest in spiritual things now became commonplace; concern for one's salvation was uppermost in that region where recently lawlessness had ruled. Other huge camp meetings were held in later months, and the area of revival soon spread into Tennessee.'" [118]

Account #8:

"At Gasper River, on the fourth Sabbath of June, a surprising multitude of people collected, many from a very great distance, even from the distance of thirty to sixty, and one hundred miles. On Friday and Saturday there was a very solemn attention.

On Saturday evening, after the congregation was dismissed, as a few serious, exercised Christians were sitting conversing together, and appeared to be more than commonly engaged, the flame started from them and overspread the whole house until every person appeared less or more engaged." [119]

Account #9:

"The Gasper River gathering was a sensational success and led instantaneously to the holding of other camp meetings along the frontier. Presbyterian and Methodist ministers alike, impressed with McGready's success, held similar services that spontaneously captured the fancy of the pioneers, who were willing to travel great distances to attend. During the summer of 1800, Presbyterians, Baptists, and Methodists united to hold one revival after another." [120]

Account #10:

"This was the first planned camp meeting. Volunteers arrived days early to cut away trees and undergrowth around the 'meetinghouse'. This was to make room for the people and the wagons that were expected. They did not anticipate what occurred. An enormous crowd, as many as several thousand, arrived at the appointed date.

Thirteen wagon loads of people and provisions showed up ready to camp out at this meeting. Whole families had come prepared to camp out for days. Some of these people had traveled over 100 miles, on wilderness roads or trails, to be there. The estimates of the number present ran as high as 8,000 men, women, and children." [121]

CHAPTER 17

 Locations of the Second Great Awakening

Muddy River Church in Logan County, Kentucky

Rev. James McGready, Pastor

Account #1:

"The Muddy River church was the scene in late September, 1799 of 'the greatest, the most solemn and powerful time of any that had been before.'" [122]

Account #2:

[John] "Rankin wrote in his autobiography that on this occasion (September, 1799) he warned the hesitant with a pertinent text: 'Behold, ye despisers and wonder.., for I work a work in your days- a work which you shall in no wise believe- though a man declare it to you.'" [123]

Account #3:

"On Sunday following this meeting [Beech Meetinghouse] a most wonderful meeting was held at Muddy River Church, a few miles north of Russellville, KY. To this meeting the people came in all kinds of vehicles, on horseback and on foot, from all distances up to 100 miles. Long before the hour for preaching came there were present three times as many as the house could seat, and still they came singly, and in companies of tens, fifties and hundreds.

A temporary pulpit was erected in the woods, and seats for the multitude made by felling large trees and laying them on the ground. 'Preaching commenced, and soon the presence of the all-pervading power was felt throughout the vast assembly. As night came on it was apparent the crowd did not intend to disperse. Some took wagons and hurried to bring in straw from barns and treading-yards. Some fell to sewing the wagon sheets together and others to cutting forks and poles on which to spread them. Counterpanes, coverlets and sheets were also fastened together to make tents or camps. Others were dispatched to town and to the nearest homes to collect bacon, meal, flour, with cooking utensils to prepare food for the multitude. In a few hours it was a sight to see how much was gathered together for the encampment. Fires were made, cooking begun, and by dark, candles were lighted and fixed to a hundred trees; and here was the first and perhaps the most beautiful camp-ground the world has ever seen.'" [124]

CHAPTER 18

Locations of the Second Great Awakening

Robert Shaw's House in Sumner County, Tennessee

This sacramental meeting apparently occurred on private land connected to the home of Robert Shaw. I have found no other references that would indicate that this was initially or became a meetinghouse for a congregation. Many times, the camp meetings would take place on land that belonged to individuals that welcomed the gathering.

Account #1:

"The great revival was underway in Sumner County in the summer of 1800, when a large number of people assembled at a sacramental meeting held at Robert Shaw's on the head waters of Red River near the Robertson County line. Those attending were quickly caught up in the spirit of the Kentucky revival as they listened to Reverend McGready of Logan County. He was assisted by Presbyterians Rankin and Craighead of Nashville, and William McGee of Shiloh, all of whom would continue to promote camp meetings during the next decade.

Years later, John McGee recalled in a letter an incident at this meeting: 'There was a man at the ridge meeting who got mad, cursed the people, and said he would go home, but before he got out of sight of the campground, a tree fell on him, and he was carried home dead.'" [125]

Account #2:

"In 1800, the revival commenced among us in Sumner County. The news of the wonderful excitement in Logan county [Kentucky], under the labors of Mr. McGready, was heard by us; and a vast multitude of people assembled at a sacramental meeting held at Robert Shaw's, on the head waters of Red river, in the summer of 1800. Messrs. McGready, McGee, and Rankin, were Presbyterian preachers who labored at that meeting. Parson Craighead [known to be an opposer of the revival] was also in attendance. Such displays of divine power as were there seen, I had never before witnessed. Under the preaching of Messrs. McGready and McGee, the people fell down like men slain in battle; and the number that professed religion [conversion] will never be known in time. The meeting lasted several days. Parson Craighead appeared to be friendly to the work." [126]

CHAPTER 19

Locations of the Second Great Awakening

Drake's Creek Meetinghouse in Sumner County, TN

The Drake's Creek Meetinghouse and its land were located in what is now Hendersonville, Tennessee. From the references I have found, it appears to have been an area of land located within what is now Sanders Ferry Park near the end of Sanders Ferry Road. At the entrance of the park, there are graves of the Sanders family and so it is reasonable to assume this is the approximate location of the meetinghouse and land for the camp meetings.

Author's Note: This is not the same location as the Presbyterian Beech Meetinghouse which was often referred to as being held on 'Drake's Creek'.

Account #1:

"[Sanders Ferry Road] was named for James Sanders, who (among other things) donated the land for the first Methodist meetinghouse in 1799. James Sanders was not related to Hubbard Saunders, for whom Saundersville is named." [127] (Hubbard Saunters also donated land for a meetinghouse in Hendersonville, near Gallatin.)

Account #2: [At the entrance of what is now Sanders Ferry Park in Hendersonville] "The cemetery & surrounding tract formerly owned by James Sanders, a prominent landholder who operated a Cumberland River ferry here.

And he also conveyed land for the Drake's Creek Meetinghouse (Methodist) which stood nearby. Substantial portions of this and the Daniel Smith (Rock Castle) tracts, once separated by Drake's Creek, were flooded by the impoundment of Old Hickory Lake in the 1950s." [128]

Account #3:

"John McGee, a Methodist minister, held the first known Tennessee camp meeting at Drake's Creek, Sumner County, in August 1800, and revivalism quickly spread throughout the fall of 1800 and into 1801." [129]

Account #4:

"Not long after the meeting at Robert Shaw's, a week-long meeting was held at Drake's Creek meetinghouse. Bishop Asbury and party arrived at the close of a sacramental solemnity, that had been held four days by Craighead, Hodge, Rankin, McGee and Adair, Presbyterian officiating ministers: We came in and Brother McKendree preached upon Jeremiah 4:14; after him, Brother Whatcoat preached upon, 'We know that we are of God'… It is supposed that there were one thousand souls present…" [130]

Account #5:

[From Francis Asbury's journal describing the same meeting] "We came by Manslick [Mansker's Lick?] to Drake's Creek meetinghouse...I also spoke; my subject was the work of God. Last Sabbath was my birthday. This will make the thirteenth year of my labours in America.

It is supposed there are one thousand souls present, and double that number heard the word of life on Sunday." [131]

Account #6:

"Soon afterward [after the camp meeting held at Robert Shaw's on the headwaters of Red River], a week-long meeting was held at Drake's Creek Meetinghouse and those present heard four Presbyterian preachers before the arrival of Methodist Bishop Francis Asbury; William McKendree, who would soon become the first American born bishop of the Methodist Church; and Richard Whatcoat, the great English preacher. One thousand were reported present at Drake's Creek." [132]

Account 7:

"[Bishop Francis] Asbury's first experience with this sort of meeting was apparently in October 1800 at Drake's Creek (in what is now Hendersonville) in the Cumberland District of Middle Tennessee (this was also apparently the earliest camp meeting in that state). He captured the flavor of the event by writing that there, in the open air,

The ministers of God, Methodists and Presbyterians, united their labours, and mingled with the child-like simplicity of primitive times. Fires blazing

here and their dispelled the darkness, and the shouts of the redeemed captives, and the cries of the precious souls struggling into life, broke the silence of midnight. The weather was delightful; as if heaven smiled, whilst mercy flowed in abundant streams of salvation to perishing sinners. We suppose there were at least thirty souls converted at this meeting. I rejoiced that God is visiting the sons of the Puritans (Presbyterians), who are candid enough to acknowledge their obligations to the Methodists.'

From that time on the bishop was an enthusiastic supporter of camp meetings, believing that "they have never been tried without success. He duly attended and reported on meetings held in every part of America.

For Asbury these [camp] meetings were 'harvest time', the reaping of precious souls that had been saved. In the early years it often meant working with Presbyterians, and that was agreeable to him as long as it furthered the objectives of Methodism.

(The bishop even admired the quality of their ministers, though a bit defensive about their generally higher level of education.) Unlike some Presbyterians, he cared not a whit that these meetings lacked sophistication or reasoned theology. It was faith that mattered!" [133]

Account #8:

[Rev. Richard Whatcoat speaking] "As we journeyed on toward Nashville, in the state of Tennessee, partly a south course of about two hundred and twenty miles, we heard a strange report about religion. We were told that the Presbyterians work by new rules; that they make the people cry and fall down, and profess to be converted. The 19th of October, William McKendree, Bishop Asbury, and myself preached at Nashville, (the capital of

Cumberland settlement, finely situated on the banks of the river) to a large assembly: the Word seemed to be with power; the 20th we attended the Presbyterian sacramental meeting, held at Montgomery Meetinghouse, on Drake Creek, which continued four days and nights.

After a short intercourse with the ministers, they desired us to take the stand, and speak to the people; accordingly brother McKendree, Bishop Asbury, and myself, spoke freely; the power of the Lord was present to wound and to heal; several found peace that evening. It was truly pleasing to see so many gathered together, under the stately beech trees, to worship and adore the great Creator and Redeemer of mankind." [134]

Account # 9:

[1800] "Yesterday, [at Drake's Creek] and especially during the night, were witnessed scenes of deep interest. Fires blazing here and there, dispelled the darkness, and the shouts of the redeemed captives, and cries of precious souls struggling into life, broke the silence of midnight. The weather was delightful; as if heaven smiled while mercy flowed in abundance streams of salvation to perishing sinners. We supposed there were at least thirty souls converted at this meeting. I rejoice that God is visiting the sons of the Puritans, who are candid enough to acknowledge their obligation to the Methodists." [135]

Account #10:

"Another example of the cooperation between Presbyterians and Methodists is described here. Shortly after the Gasper River meeting in the summer of 1800, a week long meeting was held at Drake's Creek Meetinghouse.

Asbury with his party arrived 'at the close of a sacramental solemnity that had been held four days by Craighead, Hodge, Rankin, McGee, and Adair, Presbyterian officiating ministers; Methodists McKendree and Whatcoat preached to one thousand people.'" [136]

CHAPTER 20

Locations of the Second Great Awakening

The Ridge Meetinghouse in Sumner County, TN

Pastor William McGee

One source found on the internet indicated the following information regarding the location of this Meetinghouse/camp meeting site: The Ridge Meetinghouse originally in Sumner County, Tennessee, near the line of Robertson County, TN. [137] It is said to have been about 25 miles north of Nashville and was a Presbyterian church, originally. The church was at this location until 1884, and then it became Walnut Grove Cumberland Presbyterian Church. The church relocated to Robertson County (1884-1906).

Account #1:

[In September of 1799] "the sacramental meeting at Muddy River Meetinghouse was followed by another at the Ridge, a few miles across the Tennessee border." [138]

Account #2:

"In October [of 1799] the sacrament was administered at the Ridge (a vacant congregation in western Tennessee), by McGready, McGee, and Rankin, and the revival spread to that region." [139]

Account #3:

"In September of 1800, Mr. McGready assisted Mr. [William] McGee in holding a camp meeting at The Ridge Meetinghouse." [Multitudes attended both meetings, The Ridge and Shiloh Meetinghouses, and great effects were produced.] [140]

Account #4:

"At [The] Ridge Meetinghouse Camp Meeting] Sacrament, in Cumberland [Tennessee], the second Sabbath in September, about 45 souls, we believe, obtained religion." [141]

Account #5:

"In Biographical Sketches, 1st Series, page 79, in the Life of Rev. Thos. Calhoun, is a sketch written by said Calhoun, in which he says: 'The same year my father emigrated to Tennessee, there was a camp meeting at what was called Ridge Meetinghouse, in Sumner county. My father took his family to that meeting. I was then in my 18th year [he was born May 31, 1782]. . . . We stopped about 100 yards from the pulpit where the religious exercises were going on. Many sinners were on their knees, crying for mercy. I never before heard such cries. A trembling at once seized my whole frame, so that it was with some difficulty I walked to the ground where they lay. Shortly after taking my seat, a sermon was delivered, which seemed greatly to increase the work of my conviction.'

In speaking of the mourners at said meeting, he says: 'William. McGee and Samuel King were talking to them.' Three weeks after this, Mr. Calhoun was converted at [Blythe's] Big Springs." [142]

CHAPTER 21

 Locations of the Second Great Awakening

Shiloh Meetinghouse in Sumner County, Tennessee

Originally Rev. William McGee was the Pastor,
but by 1800, it was Rev. William Hodge

"The Shiloh congregation/Shiloh Church was organized in 1793 by the Rev. William McGee from the Muhlenberg Presbytery. The first building was located on the hill between the Scottsville Pike and the Hartsville Pike on property now owned by Dr. Enoch. It set just behind his veterinarian clinic. An old cemetery now marks the spot. The church remained in this building until about 1830. McGee was the pastor of the church until about 1800." [143]

Account #1

"In September of 1800, one week after the camp meeting at The Ridge Meetinghouse] "Messrs. McGready and [William] McGee assisted Mr. Hodge in a similar meeting at Shiloh. Multitudes attended both meetings, and great effects were produced." [144]

Account #2:

"McGready's account records a continued outpouring of the revival effects at Red River the following week; at Shiloh, in Tennessee, from whence a group of young people had attended the Gasper River meeting, and at Muddy River on the fifth Sabbath in August. At the latter meeting, a vast multitude assembled from far and wide.

There were twenty-two wagons loaded with people and their provisions besides a large number of people prepared to camp on the grounds. Rankin was prominent and on Saturday preached with such effectiveness that 'Christians were filled with joy unspeakable and full of glory, and poor sinners sensibly felt the arrows of the Almighty sticking fast in their hearts.' Thus the solemnity began and continued until Tuesday morning during which time McGready thinks about fifty persons were converted from their sins. The revivalists journeyed to Tennessee for meetings at the Ridge and at Shiloh during September; at Clay-lick and Montgomery's meeting-house during October; at Little Muddy-creek (one of Rankin's congregations) and at Hopewell, in Tennessee, during November. He also mentions Drake's Creek where Rankin preached several times, and it was thought about thirty persons in that area had obtained religion." [145]

CHAPTER 22

Locations of the Second Great Awakening

Blythe's Big Spring in Sumner County, Tennessee

<u>Account #1:</u>

"In September, 1800, a revival or sacramental meeting was called to be held at Blythe's Big Spring on Desha's Creek. The news of the great meetings at Bob Shaw's and at Drake's Creek had spread throughout Cumberland County and the response at Blythe's Big Spring was overwhelming.

John McGee, the Methodist preacher and brother of Presbyterian preacher, William McGee, said that 'many thousands attended' and characterized it as 'perhaps the greatest meeting we ever witnessed in this country...' John Carr said the crowd 'comprised the largest number of people every known to be collected together in the country'.

Preaching was a joint effort of Presbyterians Rankin, McGready, Craighead and William McGee, and Methodists Sewell, Page and John McGee. The meeting lasted four days and nights and Carr reported 'scores of precious souls were brought from darkness to light and from the power of Satan to God'. John McGee wrote, 'The people fell before the Word like corn before a storm of wind, and many rose from the dust with divine glory shining in their countenances...'

One of the memorable events at Blythe's Big Spring meeting involved John Adam Grenade, a Methodist who had come across the mountains to Sumner County two years before. Grenade was reputed to be a poet and, having rejected what he regarded as a call to preach, he became deeply depressed. He would spend long periods in the woods alone, reading his Bible and calling upon God for mercy.

At the revival, Grenade 'obtained deliverance from bondage...the clergy as well as the laity were struck with wonder...Heaven was pictured on the face of the happy man...He spoke of angels and archangels...and...upon the fullness...of the gospel of Christ.' From this meeting, he went forth to become one of the most dramatic preachers of his day, serving most of his ministry in East Tennessee.

On this occasion, intense 'bodily agitations or exercises' were manifest by many present. Those affected would be seized by rapid and involuntary jerking movements or would appear to be struck dumb and fall prone on the ground. The jerking, sometimes accompanied by running, jumping or dancing, would be ended by a confession or testimonial by the person seized. There were also laughing, singing and barking exercises, all of which – even the laughing – were carried on in an atmosphere of intense solemnity. These practices spread and became commonplace at the many brush arbor revival meetings on the frontier in the early nineteenth century." [146]

Account #2:

"In the autumn, a camp meeting was held at Blythe's Big Spring on Desha's Creek and thousands attended. Three Presbyterian and three Methodist preachers shared leadership of the meeting during which intense 'bodily agitations or exercises' were manifest by many present. Those affected would be seized by rapid and involuntary jerking movements or would appear to be struck dumb and fall prone to the ground." [147]

Account #3:

"In September of the same year [1800], a sacramental meeting was appointed to be held at Shiloh; but, on account of the scarcity of water there, the appointment was changed to Blythe's Big Spring, on Desha's Creek. The news of the great work at Shaw's having spread throughout Middle Tennessee; this meeting at Blythe's comprised the largest number of people ever known to be collected together in the country.

Messrs. McGrady [McGready], McGee, and Rankin, Presbyterian preachers, and Messrs. John McGee, John Page, and John Sewell, Methodist preachers, labored at this meeting. Parson Craighead was also present.

On the first day of the meeting, the people arriving in crowds, in wagons, on horseback, and on foot, presented a wonderful scene. The preachers united their hearts and hands like a band of brothers, and the great work commenced immediately, and progressed night and day without intermission, and with increasing interest to the end.

It would be impossible to describe the scenes presented at that meeting, particularly when one saw many men, women, and children, from the aged father down to the youngest son, now stretched upon the ground and pleading for mercy; then rising, and with shouts giving glory to God. It was indeed a solemn time.

One young man, I recollect, who, having been brought under conviction, hastened to his horse, with the view of going home; but, before mounting, he fell like a man shot in battle; and he continued upon the ground until the Lord blessed his soul when he arose and gave glory to God for his deliverance. Such occurrences were very frequent.

The meeting lasted four days and nights, and scores of precious souls were brought from darkness to light and from the power of Satan to God. One family, named Sullivan, of three brothers and sisters, neighbors of mine on Goose Creek, though they had been raised Quakers, walked twelve or fourteen miles to that meeting, and all of them professed religion, and proved to be excellent members of the Church.

The Presbyterians shared largely in the fruits of the revival; and a number of young men, as well as others somewhat advanced in life, soon became convinced that they were called to preach the gospel; and they went forth as flaming heralds, proclaiming life and salvation to a lost and dying world. From that great revival sprang the Cumberland Presbyterian Church; and from that meeting the work of God spread throughout Middle TN." [148]

Account #4:

"Historian [Walter] Durham reported that in September 1800, a revival was held at Blythe's Big Spring at Desha's Creek. Thousands attended. Preaching was a joint effort of Presbyterians Rankin, McGready, Thomas Craighead, and William McGee and Methodists Sewell, John Page, and John McGee. This meeting lasted four days and nights." [149]

CHAPTER 23

 Locations of the Second Great Awakening

Walton's Campground in Sumner County, Tennessee

Account #1:

"In the fall of 1779, Mansker in company with Amos Eaton, Daniel Frazier, and 'a number of other immigrants' followed the Kentucky trail and arrived on the frozen middle Cumberland close on the heels of the party guided by Captain James Robertson, probably in January, 1780. Mansker, assisted by William Neely, Daniel Frazier, James Franklin, and others, built a fort on the west side of Mansker's Creek, located three or four hundred yards downstream from the later site of Walton's Campground." [150]

Account #2:

"Isaac Walton (1764-1840), and his brother, William Walton, were some of the first land owners in the area we now know as Goodlettsville, Tennessee. Isaac's land was adjacent to one of the plots of land belonging to Casper Mansker on which Mansker Station was built. In addition to being a wealthy land owner, Isaac was also an entrepreneur (using his home as both an inn for frontier travelers and a tavern) and was considered to be a community leader.

By 1800 religion had become a significant part of Isaac Walton's life. Methodism had penetrated the Cumberland country and by 1797 Mansker's Station was one of the preaching places on the itinerary of Benjamin Ogden, the first Methodist preacher of record in this section of Tennessee.

And sometime in 1800, most likely following these great revival meetings, Isaac Walton gave six acres of land on the Sumner County side of Mansker's Creek, near the Long Hollow Road, as a site for a campground (named Walton's Campground) and meetinghouse. A white ash log building was constructed there that measured 32' x 40'. Revivals tended to last no more than two years, but the Walton's Campground survived. In 1804, the building there was replaced by a 26' by 30' structure, which served as a place of worship for many years. Perhaps from the beginning it was Methodist by persuasion, but it was also Presbyterian, and many groups must have taken part in camp meetings at this site." [151]

Account #3:

"It (Walton's Campground) was called 'Campground' because when there was a revival at the church, people came from miles around in their wagons and with their families to camp out for the week or two the revival lasted." [152]

Account #4:

"Walton's Campground named for Isaac Walton, founded by the Methodist church about 1802, stood south of Long Hollow Road on the east bank of Mansker's Creek. Used as a place of worship until 1856, when the congregation moved to Connell Memorial Methodist Church, named for Enoch Prince Connell." [153]

Account #5:

"The Goodlettsville Cumberland Presbyterian Church was an outgrowth of the Great Revival Meetings during 1799 in Kentucky and Tennessee. In 1800, Isaac Walton donated six acres of land as a place of worship. This land was located on the east bank of Mansker's Creek on Long Hollow Pike.

This site became known as Walton's Campground. During the first half of the 19th Century, several groups held worship services at Walton's Campground." [154]

Account #6:

"Doubtless, prompted by the spread throughout the county of the great revival, Isaac Walton in 1800 gave a six-acre tract of land located on the east bank of Mansker's Creek on Long Hollow Pike in Sumner County for a meetinghouse and campground. The meetinghouse was built of white ash logs and was about thirty-two feet wide and forty feet long. 'Walton's Campground' became a familiar name throughout the Cumberland country.

When there was a revival meeting at the church, people came from miles around with their families and camped out for the term of the meeting- usually seven to fourteen days." [155]

Author's Note: I made an earnest attempt to locate a first-hand account of a camp meeting held at Walton's Campground in the early days of the awakening, but was not successful. Each expert I spoke to indicated that in all likelihood an account of this sort for this location did not exist, as many of the camp meetings were not documented.

I decided the next best thing was the following account that is describing a typical camp meeting in Tennessee, as an event at Walton's Campground would have followed this same pattern.

<u>Account #6:</u> Description of a typical camp meeting in Tennessee

"Thus the early years of the 19th century saw the memorable camp meetings in progress in the Cumberland, with people of all religious denominations participating. *Flint's Geography* contains the following interesting description of an early camp meeting in this part of Tennessee:

None but one who has seen, can imagine the interest, excited in a district of country perhaps fifty miles in extent, by the awaited approach of the time for a camp meeting; and none but one who has seen, can imagine how profoundly the preachers have understood what produces effect, and how well they have practiced upon it. Suppose the scene to be, where the most extensive excitements and most frequent camp meetings have been, during the two past years, in one of the beautiful and fertile valleys among the mountains of Tennessee. The notice has been circulated two or three months. On the appointed day, coaches, chaises, wagons, carts, people on horseback, and multitudes traveling from a distance on foot, wagons with provisions, mattresses, tents, and arrangements for the stay of a week, are seen hurrying from every point towards the central spot. It is in the midst of a grove of those beautiful and lofty trees, natural to the valleys of Tennessee, in its deepest verdure, and beside a spring branch, for the requisite supply of water.

The line of tents is pitched; and the religious city grows up in a few hours under the trees, beside the stream. Lamps are hung in lines among the branches; and the effect of their glare upon the surrounding forest is as of magic. The scenery of the most brilliant theatre in the world is a painting only for children, compared with it. Meantime the multitudes, with the highest excitement of social feeling added to the general enthusiasm of expectation, pass from tent to tent, and interchange apostolic greetings and embraces, and talk of the coming solemnities.

Their coffee and tea are prepared, and their supper is finished. By this time the moon, (for they take thought, to appoint the meeting at the proper time of the moon) begins to show its disk above the dark summits of the mountains; and a few stars are seen glimmering through the intervals of the branches. The whole constitutes a temple worthy of the grandeur of God." [156]

Author's Note: The original site of Walton's Campground was located on what is now the approximate area of North Creek Park near the intersection of Jackson Road and Long Hollow Pike in Goodlettsville.

CHAPTER 24

 Locations of the Second Great Awakening

Cane Ridge Meetinghouse in Bourbon County, KY

Barton W. Stone, Pastor

Account #1:

"Barton Stone, a pastor Cane Ridge, Kentucky, was among those in attendance. So moved was he by the outpouring of the Holy Spirit, fervent prayer, confession of sin, and powerful praise service that he invited McGready to lead a meeting at Cane Ridge in August 1801. McGready agreed." [157]

Account #2:

[After the Gasper River Meeting in Logan County, KY] "Interest in spiritual things now became commonplace; concern for one's salvation was uppermost in that region where recently lawlessness had ruled. Other huge camp meetings were held in later months, and the area of revival soon spread into Tennessee.

Yet the full force of the movement was yet to be experienced, and it came about through the activity of Barton W. Stone (1772–1844), Presbyterian pastor of the Cane Ridge and Concord churches, northeast of Lexington, Kentucky. Stone traveled to Logan County to observe McGready's work, and returned home to plan a similar meeting for August 1801 at Cane Ridge." [158]

Account #3:

"After some preliminary revivals, he [Barton Stone] announced a great meeting to be held at Cane Ridge on August 6, 1801. When the day arrived; so did a great many ministers, including some Baptists and Methodists, and an unbelievably large concourse of people. The crowd was estimated at from ten to twenty-five thousand, and this at a time when nearby Lexington, the state's largest city, barely exceeded two thousand. This 'sacramental occasions' continued for six or seven days and nights, and would have gone on longer except for the failure of provisions for such a crowd. When it was over, Cane Ridge was referred to as the greatest outpouring of the Spirit since Pentecost. It marks a watershed in American church history, and the little log meetinghouse around which the multitudes thronged and writhed has become a shrine for all who invoke 'the frontier spirit' in American Christianity.

The Cane Ridge meeting has challenged the descriptive powers of many historians, yet none has risen fully to the occasion. Critics and sensationalists then and since have dwelt exclusively on the rampant emotionalism and bodily agitations. Most of those who were caught up in the enthusiasm were never able to report it objectively. Barton Stone himself stated the basic fact: Many things transpired there, which were so much like miracles, that if they were not, they had the same effects as miracles on infidels and unbelievers; for many of them by these were convinced that Jesus was the Christ, and bowed in submission to Him. One must try to re-create the scene: the milling crowds of hardened frontier farmers, tobacco-chewing, tough-spoken, notoriously profane, famous for their alcoholic thirst; their scarcely demure wives and large broods of children; the rough clearing, the row of wagons and crude improvised tents with horses staked out behind; the gesticulating speaker on a rude platform, or perhaps simply a preacher holding forth from a fallen tree. At night, when the forest's edge was lined by the flickering light of many campfires, the effect of apparent miracles would be heightened. For men and women accustomed to retiring and rising with the birds, these turbulent nights must have been especially awe-inspiring. And underlying every other conditioning circumstance was the immense loneliness of the frontier farmer's normal life and the exhilaration of participating in so large a social occasion.

The physical effects of so drastic a conjunction of apathy and fervor, loneliness and sociality, monotony and miracle, could not have been mild. Critics thought they noted a greater increase of fleshly lust than of spirituality, and charged that *more souls were begot than saved;* while even the most sympathetic observers conceded that camp-meeting conversions were not decorous religious transactions." [159]

Account #4:

"Remarkable in the daytime, the almost incomprehensibility of the Cane Ridge revival was enormously magnified in the darkness. As a contemporary described it in awe:

'At night, the whole scene was awfully sublime. The ranges of tents, the fires, reflecting light amidst the branches of the towering trees; the candles and lamps illuminating the encampment; hundreds moving to and fro, with lights and torches, like Gideon's army; the preaching, praying, singing and shouting, all heard at once, rushing from different parts of the ground, like the sound of many waters, was enough to swallow up all the powers of contemplation. Sinners falling, and shrieks and cries for mercy awakened in the mind a lively apprehension of that scene, when the awful sound will be heard, 'Arise ye dead and come to Judgement.'" [160]

Account #5:

"Friday, August 6, 1801—wagons and carriages bounced along narrow Kentucky roads, kicking up dust and excitement as hundreds of men, women, and children pressed toward Cane Ridge, a church about 20 miles east of Lexington. They hungered to partake in what everyone felt was sure to be an extraordinary 'Communion'.

By Saturday, things were extraordinary, and the news electrified this most populous region of the state; people poured in by the thousands. One traveler wrote a Baltimore friend that he was on his way to the 'greatest meeting of its kind ever known' and that 'religion has got to such a height here that people attend from a great distance'; on this occasion I doubt not but there will be 10,000 people.'

He underestimated, but his miscalculation is understandable. Communions (annual three-to-five-day meetings climaxed with The Lord's Supper) gathered people in the dozens, maybe the hundreds. At this Cane Ridge Communion, though, sometimes 20,000 people swirled about the grounds—watching, praying, preaching, weeping, groaning, and falling. Though some stood at the edges and mocked, most left marveling at the wondrous hand of God.

Early Sunday morning, relative calm reigned, though some had been up most of the night. The central purpose of the gathering—the Communion—took place as scheduled in the meetinghouse. The minister of a nearby congregation preached the traditional sermon outside, and then those with Communion tokens went inside for the sacrament. The tables, set up in the shape of a cross in the aisles, could probably accommodate 100 at a time. Over the ensuing hours, hundreds were served. Lyle wrote that he had 'clearer views of divine things than ... before' as he partook, and that he felt 'uncommonly tender' as he spoke.

'Sinners dropping down on every hand, shrieking, groaning, crying for mercy, convoluted', one witness said, 'professors [believers] praying, agonizing, fainting, falling down in distress for sinners, or in raptures of joy! Some singing, some shouting, clapping their hands, hugging and even kissing, laughing; others talking to the distressed, to one another, or to opposers of the work, and all this at once.'

'Fatigued ministers were in constant demand to attend the slain, to pray with the distressed, and to calm the hysterical. As dark descended and the night grew late, the cacophony continued and then began to trail off. Still, some stayed up all night, grabbing sleep whenever they could, arising later for more prayer and exhortation and singing.'" [161]

"By Monday, food and supplies were running short, and appointments had to be kept, forcing many families to cut short their stay. But the momentum could not be stopped. Arrivals, some coming from great distances after hearing of the revival, continued to flood the grounds.

Ministers who had gone home to preach at their churches on Sunday returned to minister to the many people in distress.

For four more days, the singing, praying, preaching, and falling continued; slowly dribbling to a stop on Thursday.

Few could comprehend, let alone describe, what had happened. Barton Stone said, 'A particular description of this meeting would fill a large volume, and then the half would not be told.'

Nor could anyone get a handle on the numbers. Estimates of attendance ran between 10,000 and 25,000; estimates of the slain from 1,000 to 3,000; estimates of those who took Communion from 800 to 3,000; estimates of conversions, from 1,000 to 3,000." [162]

Account #6:

"Writing about one of the events of those days, Mr. [Barton] Stone relates:

A memorable meeting was held at Cane Ridge in August, 1801. The roads were crowded with wagons, carriages, horses and footmen moving to the solemn camp. It was judged that between twenty and thirty thousand persons were assembled.

Four or five preachers spoke at the same time in different parts of the encampment without confusion. The Methodists and Baptist preachers aided in the work, and all appeared cordially united in it. They were of one mind and soul. The salvation of sinners was the one object. We all engaged in singing the same songs, all united in prayer, all preached the same gospel. The numbers converted will be known only in eternity.

Many things transpired in the meeting which was so much like miracles that they had the same effect as miracles on unbelievers. By them many were convinced that Jesus was the Christ, and were persuaded to submit to Him.

This meeting would have continued longer, but food for such a multitude failed. To this meeting many had come from Ohio and other distant parts. These returned home and diffused the same spirit in their respective neighborhoods, and similar results followed. So low had religion sunk, and such carelessness had universally prevailed, I had thought that nothing common could have arrested and held the attention of the people." [163]

"One day amidst the place
where my dear God has been,
is sweeter than ten thousand days
of pleasurable sin."

From a song entitled, *Little Marlborough*
written in 1763 by Isaac Watts

CHAPTER 25

 First-Hand Accounts

Account #1:

"Then suddenly, about the year 1799, the atmosphere changed dramatically. In that year a Presbyterian pastoral letter stated that although there was still much immorality and vice...

'We have heard from different parts the glad tidings of the outpourings of the Spirit, and of times of refreshing from the presence of the Lord. . . . From the east, from the west, and from the south, have these joyful tidings reached our ears.'

They expressed still greater joy in 1801:

'Revivals, of a more or less general nature, have taken place in many parts, and multitudes have been added to the church. From the west, the Assembly has received intelligence of the most interesting nature. On the borders of Kentucky and Tennessee, the influences of the Spirit of God seem to have been manifested in a very extraordinary manner.'" [164]

Account #2:

"Presbyterian Barton W. Stone, pastor of the Concord and Cane Ridge churches, traveled to witness one of these revivals [In Logan County] for himself. He returned in that spring of 1801 overwhelmed.

'The scene to me was new and passing strange. ... Many, very many fell down, as men slain in battle, and continued for hours together in an apparently breathless and motionless state—sometimes for a few moments reviving, and exhibiting symptoms of life by a deep groan, or piercing shriek, or by a prayer for mercy most fervently uttered. With astonishment did I hear men, women, and children declaring the wonderful works of God.'" [165]

Account #3:

In his [John Carr's] book, *Early Times in Middle Tennessee* tells of a great spiritual revival of Presbyterians and Methodists that swept through southern Kentucky and the Cumberland Country about 1799, which was begun by the Reverend McGready, a Presbyterian minister.

"The unity of these denominations was so close, that one could not tell which was praising God the loudest or most. Nothing like the brotherly fellowship between the people had ever been known before. They worked together to build a meetinghouse. When it was finished, they asked me to name the church. Of course, I proudly named it Union Church..." [166]

Account #4:

[Barton Stone speaking] "Of the thousands of similar cases, I will mention one: At a meeting, two [worldly] young ladies, sisters, were standing together, attending the exercises and preaching at the same time, when instantly they both fell with a shriek of distress, and lay for more than an hour apparently in a lifeless state. Their mother, a pious Baptist, was in great distress, fearing they would not revive.

At length they began to exhibit signs of life, by crying fervently for mercy, and then relapsed into the same death-like state, with an awful gloom on their countenances; after a while, the gloom on the face of one was succeeded by a heavenly smile, and she cried out, 'Precious Jesus!' and spoke of the glory of the gospel to the surrounding crowd in language almost super-human, and exhorted all to repentance. In a little while after, the other sister was similarly exercised. From that time they became remarkably pious members of the Church.

I have seen very many pious persons fall in the same way, from a sense of danger of their unconverted children, brothers, or sisters, or from a sense of danger of their neighbors in a sinful world. I have heard them agonizing in tears, and strongly crying for mercy to be shown to sinners, and speaking like angels all around." [167]

[In reference to those affected by the jerking exercise] "I have inquired of those thus affected if they could not account for it, but some have told me that those were among the happiest seasons of their lives. I have seen some wicked persons thus affected, and all the time cursing the jerks, while they were thrown to the earth with violence. Though so awful to behold, I do not remember that any one of the thousands I have seen thus affected ever sustained any injury in body. This was as strange as the exercise itself.

[In reference to those affected by the barking exercise] This name of barking seems to have had its origin from an old Presbyterian preacher of East Tennessee. He had gone into the woods for private devotions, and was seized with the jerks. Standing near a sapling, he caught hold of it to prevent his falling; and, as his head jerked back, he uttered a grunt, or a kind of noise similar to a bark, his face being turned upwards. Some wag discovered him in this position, and reported that he had found the old preacher barking up a tree.

[In reference to those affected by the running exercise] I knew a young physician, of a celebrated family, who came some distance to a big meeting to see the strange things he had heard of. He and a young lady had sportively agreed to watch over and take care of each other if either should fall. At length, the physician felt something very uncommon, and started from the congregation to run into the woods. He was discovered running as for life, but did not proceed far until he fell down, and lay until he submitted to the Lord, and afterwards became a zealous member of the Church. Such cases were common." [168]

"'Thus have I,' says Mr. Stone, 'given a brief account of the wonderful things that appeared in the great excitement in the beginning of this century. That there were many eccentricities and much fanaticism in this excitement was acknowledged by its warmest advocates. Indeed, it would have been a wonder if such things had not appeared in the circumstances of that time. Yet the good effects were seen and acknowledged in every neighborhood, and among the different sects. It silenced contention and promoted unity for a while.'" [169]

Account #5:

[Testimony of Peter Cartwright, a popular evangelical Methodist minister] 'From 1801 for years a blessed revival of religion spread through almost the entire inhabited parts of the West, Kentucky, Tennessee, the Carolinas, and many other parts, especially through the Cumberland country, which was so called from the Cumberland River, which headed and mouthed in Kentucky, but in its great bend circled south through Tennessee, near Nashville. The Presbyterians and Methodists in a great measure united in this work, met together, prayed together, and preached together.

In this revival our camp meetings originated and in both these denominations they were held every year, and, indeed, have been ever since, more or less. They would erect their camps with logs or frame them, and cover them with clapboards or shingles. They would also erect a shed, sufficiently large to protect five thousand people from wind and rain, and cover it with boards or shingles; build a large stand, seat the shed, and here they would collect together from forty to fifty miles around, sometimes further than that. Ten, twenty, and sometimes thirty ministers, of different denominations, would come together and preach night and day, four or five days together; and, indeed, I have known these camp-meetings to last three or four weeks, and great good resulted from them. I have seen more than a hundred sinners fall like dead men under one powerful sermon, and I have seen and heard more than five hundred Christians all shouting aloud the high praises of God at once; and I will venture to assert that many happy thousands were awakened and converted to God at these camp-meetings. Some sinners mocked, some of the old dry professors opposed, some of the old starched Presbyterian preachers preached against these exercises, but still the work went on and spread almost in every direction, gathering additional force, until our country seemed [to be] all coming home to God." [170]

Account #6:

Ecroy Claxton's eyewitness account:

"The noise was like the roar of Niagara. The vast sea of human beings seemed to be agitated as if by storm. I counted seven ministers, all preaching at one time...Some of the people were singing, others praying, some crying for mercy in the most piteous accents, while others were shouting most vociferously...

I stepped up on to a log...The scene...was indescribable. At one time I saw at least five hundred swept down in a moment as if a battery of thousands had been opened upon them, and then immediately followed shrieks and shouts that rent the heavens."[171]

Account #7:

"'What is truly a matter of praise, wonder and gratitude to every follower of Christ,' McGready concluded of the intense revivals of 1800, 'is, that every sacramental occasion in all our congregations, during the whole summer and fall, was attended with the tokens of the sweet presence and power of the Almighty Jesus.'...By 1803, even more immersed in these ecstatic Communions, McGready could only marvel at 'God's power and presence' at these occasions. 'So many souls happy in the love of God, I never saw upon the earth before,' he exulted over the Red River sacrament in 1803. 'The exercise at the tables [Communion] was indeed a heaven upon earth. Christians at the tables, almost universally, from the first to last, were so filled with joy unspeakable, and full of glory, that they might, with propriety, be compared to bottles filled with new wine.'

The glories of these occasions had come to resemble for McGready the descent of the New Jerusalem." [172]

Account #8:

Among those in the audience were some detractors, of whom Robert W. Finley was one, even though he was the son of the builder of the Cane Ridge Meetinghouse, Rev. James B. Finley. (James B. was also a successful circuit rider who had a powerful ministry among the Wyandot Indians of Ohio.) This is what he [Robert] had to say of the events:

"On the way to the meeting I said to my companions, 'If I fall, it must be by physical power, and not by singing and praying,' and as I prided myself upon my manhood and courage, I had no fear of being overcome by any nervous excitability or being frightened into religion. We arrived upon the ground, and here a scene presented itself to my mind not only novel and unaccountable, but awful beyond description. A vast crowd, supposed by some to have amounted to twenty-five thousand, was collected together...

The vast sea of human beings. I counted seven ministers, all preaching at one time; some on stumps, others in wagons, and one - the Reverend William Burke, now of Cincinnati - was standing on a tree which had in falling lodged against another. Some of the people were singing, others praying, some crying for mercy in the most piteous accents, while others were shouting most vociferously.

While witnessing these scenes a peculiarly strange sensation, such as I had never before felt, came over me. My heart beat tumultuously, my knees trembled, my lips quivered, and I felt as though I must fall to the ground. I became so weak and powerless that I found it necessary to sit down.

Soon after I left and went into the woods, and there I strove to rally and man up my courage. I tried to philosophize in regard to these wonderful exhibitions, resolving them into mere sympathetic excitement, a kind of religious enthusiasm, inspired by songs and eloquent harangues. My pride was wounded, for I had supposed that my mental and physical strength and vigor could most successfully resist these influences.

After some time, I returned to the scene of excitement, the waves of which, if possible, had risen still higher. The same awfulness of feeling came over me. I stepped upon a log, where I could have a better view of the surging sea of humanity. The scene that then presented itself to my mind was indescribable. At one time I saw at least five hundred swept down in a moment, as if a battery of a thousand guns had been opened upon them, and then immediately followed shrieks and shouts that rent the very heavens. My hair rose up on my head, my whole frame trembled, the blood ran cold in my veins, and I fled for the woods a second time, and wished I had stayed at home.

In this state I wandered about from place to place, in and around the encampment. At times it seemed as if all the sins I had ever committed in my life were vividly brought up in array before my terrified imagination, and under their awful pressure I felt as if I must die if I did not get relief. My heart was so proud and hard that I would not have fallen to the ground for the whole State of Kentucky. I felt that such an event would have been an everlasting disgrace and put a final quietus on my boasted manhood and courage.

Then came from my streaming eyes the bitter tears and I could scarcely refrain from screaming aloud. Night approaching, we put up near Mayslick, the whole of which was spent by me in weeping and promising God if he would spare me till morning I would pray and try to mend my life and abandon my wicked courses.'"

Robert Finley went on to become a lifelong minister of some importance in the Methodist Church. [173]

Account #9:

According to James McGready:

"'...even exemplary Christians and little children were filled with a sense of guilt and awakened to the love of Christ.' Concerning the latter, McGready continues:

'I have likewise stood present, when the light of the knowledge of the glory of God in the face of Jesus broke into their souls [the children] and to the astonishment of all around them, these little creatures have started to their feet, and told all present their sweet views of the lovely, precious Jesus what fullness, sufficiency, suitableness and willingness that they saw in Him to hear them describe the sweet plan of salvation, and pointing of the nature of believing or coming to Christ to save the very worst of sinners--to hear them tell the tender, bleeding concern they felt for poor sinners: I say, to hear them speak upon these subjects, the good language, the good sense, the clear ideas, and the rational, scriptural light in which they spoke, truly amazed me. I felt mortified and mean before them. They spoke upon these subjects beyond what I could have done: an evident demonstration that, out of the mouths of babes and sucklings, the Lord can perfect praise.'" [174]

Account #10:

[This account describes a prayer offered by Richard Whatcoat as described by one that was present in the meeting. Whatcoat was a close friend of Francis Asbury and fellow preacher of the Gospel.]

"When he prayed it seemed as if he had one hand hold of heaven and the other of earth, and he brought them together. As he prayed he cried: 'Power, power! Now, Lord, Send the power!' and the power did come. O, what a stream of power came down! Not a stream, but it was like a cloud breaking and inundating the earth.

The cloud of mercy broke, and showers of blessings descended on our heads. Such shouts I never heard before, making the temple resound with their 'songs of joy and shouts of triumph. Jehovah abundantly blessed her [the church's] provision, and He satisfied her poor with bread; her priests He clothed with salvation and her saints shouted aloud for joy.'

Such is the testimony of one who was present.

'When the old warrior [Bishop Richard Whatcoat] related it to me his face shone, and his eye was moistened with a tear.'" [175]

"The Wesleyans [Methodists] were neither scandalized
nor stopped by the manifest presence of the Spirit
in their meetings. They institutionally absorbed what Jonathan
Edwards had preached, that the activity of the Holy Spirit on the
human soul and body sometimes produces disruptive
phenomena, but that such phenomena
should neither be encouraged nor suppressed.

...the Wesley brothers [John & Charles] provided leadership
that was open to the Spirit's direction even if it stretched
conventional understanding of propriety and ministry..."[176]

CHAPTER 26

 Impact & Consequences

Account #1:

"However, though camp meetings were sometimes the scenes of excesses, they were much more the scenes of great spiritual awakening. The rough, violent, irreligious frontier, which many felt threatened to undo the morals of the new nation, was being tamed by the Lamb of God." [177]

Account #2:

"This unusually widespread revival fervor gave Kentucky a special image in the eyes of the faithful everywhere. Letters poured out of Kentucky, bearing the news of an apparently unprecedented flood of revival success. As these communications, along with amazed travelers, filtered back through the rest of the South, the revival began to appear in state after state. This was to be the Great Revival of the South." [178]

Account #3:

"The Revival of 1800 (or the Great Revival, as the Second Great Awakening is sometimes called) saved the nation from moral disaster in one of the most critical periods of its history. It was brought about, not through the plans and programs of church leaders, but by the simple means of united, persistent, prevailing prayer, and the Spirit-empowered preaching of the Word.

The great doctrines of redemption were emphasized; the cardinal truths of the sovereignty of God, the holiness of His law, the deep depravity of the human soul, and the sufficiency of redemptive grace, through the atoning death of Christ, to pay the debt of sin. These were the key truths used of the Spirit of God to bring conviction of sin, and repentance to life. There were no outstanding leaders, as in the earlier revival [First Great Awakening]; but many humble men, pastors in their own parishes were the human channels of divine power. The work bore all the marks of a work of God. Neither human logic nor eloquence, but divine power alone wrought the glorious change, bringing hardened sinners and sneering sceptics alike, in deep repentance to the foot of the cross, crying: 'What must we do to be saved?'

The blessed effects of the awakening were felt throughout the nation. The whole moral tone of America was lifted to a new level. Communities which formerly were notorious for immorality, profanity, drunkenness and Sabbath desecration now were completely reformed. Drunkards and infidels [Infidelity was a type of atheism imported to America by France] were converted and became men of prayer and holiness. The frontiers of the west [Kentucky & Tennessee], once so wild and dissolute, now were become models of sobriety and morality."[179]

Account #4:

"Initially bitter rivals, the Methodist & Presbyterians, worked together during the beginnings of the move of God and the camp meetings. The Presbyterians generally were bitter persecutors of the Methodists. They called them 'enthusiasts'; and some went so far as to say they were the false prophets that were to arise in the last days.

[As a result of the move of God at Red River Meetinghouse] All prejudice and bad feeling seemed to cease between the Presbyterians and the Methodists; and it was no easy matter to tell which of them were the more noisy [noisier] in shouting the praises of God." [180]

[It was] ... "an incipient ecumenicity. At the camp meetings eight to ten ministers of different denominations would position themselves around the grounds. Presbyterian, Methodist and Baptist preachers would be present and preach at the same time at the same camp meeting." [181]

Account #5:

"In 1800, a self-sacrificing spirit of cooperation temporarily overwhelmed doctrinal rivalry, and a bond developed between Methodist and Presbyterian preachers in Sumner County, Tennessee and Logan County, Kentucky nearby. This had begun when [James] McGready asked the visiting John and William McGee to preach at Red River in Kentucky. Recall that at this meeting Methodist John McGee, with his uniquely Methodist preaching style elicited a profound emotional response among the Presbyterian worshippers." [182]

Account #6:

"...the two great legacies, the camp meeting revivals and the circuit riding evangelist, had recorded a blessed impact on the history of American Christianity." [183]

Account #7:

"It was difficult for the Presbyterians to supply the increased number of ministers required by the converts of the Great Revival. This church insisted upon an educated and trained ministry. Therefore, a few Presbyterians formed an association called 'Cumberland Presbytery,' in 1802 chiefly for the purpose of ordaining to the ministry some young men who had no classical education." [184]

"This action initiated a rift between the two, which resulted in the dismissal of the Cumberland Presbytery from the regular Presbyterian Church in 1809.

The Cumberland Presbyterians cast off the 'hifalutin' airs of the Presbyterians and incorporated language that common farmers easily understood. Cumberland ministers filled their sermons with stories shaped by the realities of life in the hinterland, and often rolled up their shirt sleeves and worked alongside their parishioners at barn raisings and corn shuckings." [185]

The Baptists separated themselves from the camp meetings over the issue of baptism.

The Methodists- who were known to love a good shout and actually enjoyed what others considered emotionalism- picked up and ran (or in the case of the circuit riders, galloped) spreading the fire that was kindled in the awakening.

Account #8:

"The [First] Great Awakening of the 1700's shaped the character of the emerging nation, but the [Second] Great Awakening of the camp meetings renewed and energized the church. This awakening combated deism. It turned many back to core religious and spiritual values, long held by Christians in the American colonies.

Alcoholism, gambling, and prostitution abated. The abolition movement received a huge boost that lasted until the 1860s." [186]

Account #9:

"The Second Great Awakening had a greater effect on society than any other revival in America...

The Second Great Awakening resulted in the establishment of numerous societies to aid in spreading the gospel, including the American Bible Society (1816), American Board of Commissioners for Foreign Missions (1810), American Sunday School Union (1817), American Tract Society (1826), and the American Home Missionary Society (1826)." [187]

Account #10: Music birthed out of revival:

"Music and hymns came to be [a] way [a] congregation learned theology. In an environment where there were no opportunities for education, few books, and most did not know how to read, songs could be easily memorized. [188] [Sacred Harp singing is a tradition of sacred choral music that originated in the American South of the United States.

The name is derived from The Sacred Harp, a ubiquitous and historically important tune book printed in shape notes.]" [189].

Account #11:

According to Wilson-Dickson, "The final moments of camp meetings literally broke down the barriers that kept blacks and whites apart. Joint worship followed with a free exchange of Christian music in a final march around the camp." [190]

Account #12:

"Rev. William Hodge removed [relocated] to Tennessee in the spring… During the summer of that year, he was invited by the Shiloh [Presbyterian] congregation to succeed Mr. [William] McGee in the pastoral office, which he accepted. Here this zealous minister of Jesus Christ had again to encounter difficulties of a very serious nature. As immediately upon the appearance of the Revival [1800], his congregation became divided into two parties: the one the warm friends of that glorious work, and the other its violent opposers. Those who opposed the work, claimed to be the majority, took possession of the church, and closed the doors against Mr. Hodge and his friends. The affair was taken before the Presbytery, which decided in favor of Mr. Hodge and the revival party. The others became highly offended, withdrew from the care of the Presbytery, formed themselves into a distinct society, called the orderly part of Shiloh Presbyterian congregation, and called Thomas B. Craighead, the staunch opposer of the revival and the measures of the revival members, as their pastor." [191]

Account #13:

"An atmosphere of recreation and spiritual renewal permeated the revivals. It is not surprising that camp meetings were marked by extreme emotional and physical 'exercises', with participants shouting, jerking, barking, falling down, or dancing about in spiritual ecstasy. Lorenzo Dow, a famous itinerant frontier evangelist, described the jerking exercises he witnessed while preaching at Knoxville. Dow noted that these spiritual exercises affected men and women of various ages, races, and economic levels." [192]

Account #14:

"William McKendree, bishop of the Western Conference of the Methodist Church, embraced the camp meeting style and systematized the method. The camp meeting method worked in tandem with the Methodist system of circuits and led to rapid expansion of Methodism in Tennessee in the early nineteenth century. In addition, the camp meeting's emphasis on repentance and grace worked well with the Methodist Arminian theology. The Methodists continued to hold camp meetings through the 1840s, long after the Baptists and Presbyterians had abandoned the outdoor revivals. Eventually 'protracted meetings', held in established meetinghouses, and almost completely replaced the camp meetings." [193]

"The Spirit of God
appears in powerful operation,
among all denominations." [194]

From a letter dated, March 19, 1801.

CHAPTER 27

 Opposition & Division

Account #1: Opposition due to doctrine.

"Among the first preachers who came to Tennessee were two eminent Presbyterian- Samuel Doak, who settled in East Tennessee, and Thomas B. Craighead, who settled in the neighborhood of Nashville, in what is now called Middle Tennessee. Both were men of deep learning and pure lives, and both were very strict in their faith and held rigidly to the doctrines of the Presbyterian Church. They especially abhorred any display of feeling or unnecessary fervor on the part of a preacher. They held with peculiar tenacity to the doctrine that God foresees and foreordains all who are to be saved and all who are not to be saved, without any exercise of will on their part. This abhorrence of manifestations of feeling, and insistence upon the fullest acceptance of the doctrine of predestination, raised a spirit of opposition that finally led to the establishment of the Cumberland Presbyterian Church [1809], and out of this division in the Presbyterian Church came the opportunity for the growth and expansion of the Methodist Church."[195]

Thomas Craighead was born in North Carolina, and studied theology and graduated from Nassau College, but moved to Davidson County, Tennessee to establish the first Presbyterian Church in Middle or West Tennessee. He opposed the great revival of 1800.

Account #2: Opposition due to physical exercises.

"While I am on this subject I will relate a very serious circumstance which I knew to take place with a man who had the jerks at a camp-meeting, on what was called the Ridge, in William Magee's congregation. There was a great work of religion in the encampment. The jerks were very prevalent. There was a company of drunken rowdies who came to interrupt the meeting. These rowdies were headed by a very large, drinking man. They came with their bottles of whisky in their pockets. This large man cursed the jerks, and all religion. Shortly afterward he took the jerks, and he started to run, but he jerked so powerfully he could not get away. He halted among some saplings, and, although he was violently agitated, he took out his bottle of whisky, and swore he would drink the damned jerks to death; but he jerked at such a rate he could not get the bottle to his mouth, though he tried hard. At length he fetched a sudden jerk, and the bottle struck a sapling and was broken to pieces, and spilled his whisky on the ground. There was a great crowd gathered round him, and when he lost his whisky he became very much enraged, and cursed and swore very profanely, his jerks still increasing. At length he fetched a very violent jerk, snapped his neck, fell, and soon expired, with his mouth full of cursing and bitterness." [196]

Account #3: Strong opposition from Anti-Revivalists.

"Some worshippers collapsed into a comatose state for hours. Some exhibited uncontrollable jerking of their head and shoulders. Others interrupted the service with loud wails and screams.

Anti-revivalist Presbyterians especially, were darkly suspicious of the source of such behavior in a worship service. Some anti-revivalist preachers ventured comments that the force possessing persons exhibiting uncontrollable, bizarre behaviors was evil itself. Some felt that particular actions at best crossed an imaginary line into the domain of appalling, sacrilegious athletics. These querulous observers realized that reports of these behaviors could make their denomination the object of public ridicule, especially by more educated or worldly individuals." [197]

Account #4: Division within the Presbyterians.

"New churches and new congregations appearing from 1800 to 1861 clearly demonstrated the importance that Tennesseans attached to organized religion. Although much of the momentum for these churches had come from the 'great revival,' doctrinal differences contributed to the creation of some of them. Other divisive factors, such as the disagreement in the Presbyterian Church over the educational qualifications for their ministers, led to the organization of the Cumberland Presbyterians in 1811. The congregation at Beech immediately became the cornerstone of Cumberland Presbyterianism in Middle Tennessee." [198]

Account #5: Groups that opposed the Revival.

"Now I will state something of the opposition that these [camp meetings] met with. As I have said before, all denominations of Christians, except the Cumberland Presbyterians, opposed them with their power, and publicly preached against them. They seem determined to put them down.

There were a great many who thought it would have disgraced their wife or daughter forever, if they had stayed on the camp-ground all night.

Besides all this, camp-meetings had other great and sore oppositions to contend with. Armed and drunken mobs of men always attended: they would saunter through the camp-ground, swearing that they would knock any man down that would interrupt them. They always had kegs and jugs of liquor hid out. Sometimes, after the congregation had left the stand, they would get into the altar and one of them would preach and the rest would cry, 'Amen!' and thus they would go on till the guard would go and disperse them, if they could; for sometimes they were too strong. In that case they would have to take their own way.

After they would get done preaching, they would bark and howl, till just before day, then they would sneak off until night again. Sometimes the horses [belonging to those attending the camp meetings] would be turned out of the pastures into the cornfields, with many of their manes and tails trimmed. Saddles cut to pieces, bridles cup up, horses stolen, carriages injured." [199]

Account #6: Strong opposition to McGready and his revivalist teachings.

"In the summer of 1798, there was a very general spiritual move among McGready's three congregations. Two Presbyterian ministers, however, who were opposed to the teachings of Mr. McGready, visited the members of his congregations and cast all the doubt that they could upon McGready's teachings that God would bring revival as a result of prayer, and that every real

Christian could and should know by the witness of the Holy Spirit that they were saved. One of these men found a church member of McGready's to assist him, and they worked diligently, teaching and speaking against James McGready's ideas with everyone who would listen. These two were successful for a time in stopping the move that God had begun.

They turned so many members of the Red River Congregation against McGready that the trustees of the church are said to have padlocked the doors of the meetinghouse so that he could not preach. Arriving at the meetinghouse and finding the doors padlocked, but with a small number of people gathered and wishing to hear him preach anyway, James McGready began to preach. As he spoke, a loud snap was heard. The padlock had broken and fallen from the door. After this, the anti-revival party was in great disarray and no one dared padlock the doors again. James McGready did not mention the padlocked door in his accounts of the revival, but he did mention the opposition, which for a time quenched the revival." [200]

Account #7: Baptist Church prosecutes a pastor who attended another denomination's revival service.

"He [Clifton Allen] moved to Sumner County, TN just prior to 14 Sept. 1799 when he purchased 640 acres from Daniel Burford, said deed stating 'land where on Allen now lives.' On the same day he purchased another tract of 17-3/4 acres on the middle fork of Station Camp Creek. He evidently sold this land but the deeds are unrecorded.

During the time that he owned this land on middle fork of Station Camp Creek, he was the pastor of El Bethel Baptist Church, near present city of Gallatin. He was a presbyter present when the Dixon Creek Baptist Church was constituted on 8 March 1800 at the home of Grant Allen in Smith County. That year he went to the great revival at Blythe's Big Spring on Desha Creek and took Communion with the Presbyterians and Methodists.

This was against the rules of the Baptist Church and he was brought to trial for so doing, but before being turned out, he resigned from the Baptist Church. *Early Times in Middle Tennessee*, by John Carr, tells this story. Soon after this he organized a Methodist Church near Bethpage called 'Mabry's Meetinghouse."[201]

Account #8:

"He [Barton Stone] labored almost night and day, and many were added to the Church. There were four or five other Presbyterian preachers that joined him in the great reformation. They preached free salvation to a dying world, and leveled their artillery against the doctrine of election and reprobation. They declared that Christ had tasted death for every man, and invited the whole world to come unto Jesus and be saved. It was not long before the anti-revival party [Presbyterians opposing the revival] saw their Confession of Faith was in danger.

The first one they brought to an account for preaching against the Confession of Faith was Richard McNemar. He was led before a Presbytery, and his case was carried up to the Synod at Lexington, Kentucky.

That body [the Synod] appeared generally very hostile to their doctrine, and there was much spirited altercation among them. The other four of the revival party expected their fate in the decision on McNemar's case. They were John Dunlary, Robert Marshal, John Thompson, and Barton W. Stone. It had been plainly hinted to them that they would not be forgotten by the Synod. So they waited anxiously for the issue until they plainly saw it would be against them all.

Then, in a short recess of the Synod, the five above-named withdrew to a private garden, where, after prayer for direction, and a free conversation with each other, they drew up a protest against the proceedings of the Synod in McNemar's case, and a declaration of their independence, and of their withdrawal from their jurisdiction, but not from their Communion. This protest they immediately presented to the Synod through the Moderator.

It was altogether unexpected by them, and produced very unpleasant feelings, and a profound silence for a few minutes - ensued. The Protestants retired to a friend's house in town, and were quickly followed by a committee of Synod to reclaim them to their standards. They had with them a very friendly conversation, the result of which was that one of the committee, Matthew Houston, became convinced that the doctrine they preached was true; and soon afterward united with them.

The committee reported to the Synod a failure to reclaim them, and after a few more vain attempts, they proceeded to the solemn work of suspending them, because they had departed from the Confession of Faith of their Church. They insisted, however, that after they had protested and withdrawn in an orderly manner, the Synod had no better right to suspend them than the Pope of

Rome had to suspend Luther after he had done the same thing; and they contended that if Luther's suspension was valid, then the whole Protestant succession was out of order." [202]

Account #9:

"Critics pointed out these examples of unseemly or antisocial behavior and denounced the camp meetings as extreme, if not dangerous, events that diverted attention away from true spirituality and religion toward more lustful pursuits. The controversies that accompanied these critiques divided some congregations along revivalist and non-revivalist lines, or along Calvinist and Arminian theological lines, and led to schism among many established congregations." [203]

Account #10: Post Mortem of the Second Great Awakening.

"Though the Great Revival died, it did not die a natural death. It was put to death by Christians who placed other things; self, denominational beliefs, often doctrine, above God." [204]

"McGready continued, till his death,
to urge all who would listen
to pray for awakening again.
He promised them, he said,
'that the work had been made easier,
because where people had received
an outpouring of God's Spirit in power,
it would make it easier to get another outpouring'.
He urged people to not move away, not to give up,
but to pray continually for another such move." [205]

CHAPTER 28

 The Coming Great Awakening

The following are prophetic words that were given by believers in the 1800's regarding another Great Awakening that they believed was coming to America sometime after the year 2000:

"Some of McGready's followers in the Red River area, continued, even after his death, to pray for that revival. Some of them said that God assured them that another great outpouring would come, and that this time it would be world-wide. They also said that they were assured that it would not come in their time, but farther into the future. It would be followed, they said, by a time worse than anything America had ever experienced. Some of these people had, only a few years before, experienced an Indian war. They said that what would come would make that warfare and those times seem pale by comparison.

James McGready began to say before his death (which was in 1817), that God had assured him, too, that there would be another great outpouring. He said it would come near the end of the age.

It was declared that it would come sometime after the year 2000, and would be followed swiftly by the worst times that America had ever seen. The horrible times that would follow would come as a judgement on the church of America, for though many would repent and be converted in that awakening, the church as a whole would not change, and the church of that time would be in great need of repentance.

Their sins would be complacency, conformity to the world system, love of money and material things, and a seeking after such things, rather than seeking after God.

The church of that day and age would say many things, but it would only be parroting what most of the world was saying. Their service would not be unto God, but unto men, and therefore would count for nothing. They would talk much of loving their fellow man, but love of God would not be practiced. The two cardinal rules for the church of that day and time would seem to be how they acted toward their fellow men, as exemplified and expected by Caesar, and how much material gain they amassed. In becoming like the world system, Christians of that day would assure themselves that they were pleasing to God, though they would actually be far from pleasing Him.

When the revival came, most of these Christians would not change, but would only entrench themselves in the above sins, and would take and claim the revival as merely their due from God. Acting as if, and even claiming, that God had sent the revival to benefit them, they would take it as a stamp of approval on their ways, and would become more hardened than ever, refusing even to consider that they might be in sin and need of change.

As many had successfully done to The Great Revival and to all other revivals, they would attempt to take this new move of God hostage to their own perverse purposes, and use it for their own glory and to further their own agenda.

The horrible judgement that would come would be merely their just due." [206]

"Perhaps what has happened is that the 'best' –

revival plus The Lord's Supper – has been hidden

for a season for another purpose.

In other words, the best in the kingdom of God

happens when what was eliminated is restored

and added to what substituted it."

William L. De Arteaga
Forgotten Power:
The Significance of The Lord's Supper in Revival

Some Closing Thoughts

I began this project with great determination in a valiant attempt to document a Second Great Awakening camp meeting in my own city of Goodlettsville, Tennessee at Walton's Campground. I am now in the final stages of completing this project without being successful in that endeavor. But as it turns out, I have discovered an even more priceless treasure that has been hidden for generations: The Table of the LORD!

I am now convinced that one element absent from our experience is the manner in which we celebrate what we call Communion or The Lord's Supper. As it was with those we have read about in the camp meetings, the importance of the celebration of The Table of the LORD, and the immense part it plays in any sustained move of God in the past cannot be overstated. This is entirely different, and not to be confused with the ritual of Communion celebrated in our day.

We must consider that a component is lacking in our corporate worship. We sing and give praises to God together in song, and that is absolutely appropriate. But, I think we have made an error in believing that the only way we get to experience the Presence of God is during or after a particularly inspiring time of musical worship. What about the opportunity of worshipping together at His Table and expecting His Presence come in that setting?

We know what inspires us. What inspires Him?

We know what draws us. What draws Him?

We cannot, we dare not expect Him to come on our terms. Revival is not about us! Awakening is not about us! It is all about Him. It is about what Moses received when he cried out to the Lord to show him His glory. It is about all of the goodness of God passing by us! It is about His eternal glory being displayed!

What welcomes Him? If we believe that the Lord wants to be near His people, and we know He does, what are we missing?

That question has come to my mind so many times since I began writing this book. Have we lost something in how we both view and celebrate what we call Communion, and unknowingly through tradition substituted a counterfeit in its place? I now believe the answer to that question is an unequivocal, "Yes! Yes! Yes!" To simply use Communion as an abbreviated memorial of the death of the Lord Jesus is honorable, but incomplete. At The Last Supper, Jesus was not just preparing the disciples for His death; He was proclaiming the New Covenant in His blood that was coming as a result of His sacrificial death. So in Communion, we do not just "remember" His death, we must consider as believers the implications of what the sacrifice of the Lamb of God means to us personally and corporately as a body. In order to do that we must join together in a more communal setting just as you would at a meal sitting around an actual table.

At the beginning of February (2016), as I was preparing to speak at a class on the subject of Communion, I invited the Holy Spirit to speak to me and teach me about this celebration from His perspective so I would know what to share. What followed was an avalanche of some pretty innovative thoughts that came in the form of a flood of words over a period of days. I am still absolutely stunned at His response to my request for His opinion.

What I heard was a perspective on what I have known as Communion that was entirely new to me! If I was indeed hearing from Him, and I believe I was, I was shocked by some of the things I heard (the first of which was confirmed by the wisdom of Rev. William J. Morford, translator of the One New Man Bible).

Here are just a few:

- The Table of the LORD cannot be understood without "studying and understanding the connection it shares with the Seder (Passover meal) and Exodus 6:6, 7". [207]

- The Table of the LORD is the perfect place to remember how God raised up a Deliverer for each of us that rescued us from a life of slavery in our own personal Egypt. The story that once belonged only to the children of Israel is now the personal testimony of every believer. All because of the love of God shown to each of us in our deliverance purchased by the blood of the sacrifice of the perfect Passover Lamb for our sin.

- The Table of the LORD is the foundation for spiritual warfare, and is where we both learn about and receive the weapons and the armor of God. Here we learn about war and about a victory that has already been won. (Psa. 23:5)

- The Table of the LORD is where we grasp the reality that true unity within the body of Christ is a mighty weapon! We can learn about unity only within the context of comm*unity*. It is there we commune together. And we also learn that the body of Christ is much bigger than our little church. It is a huge body made up of believers all around the world. We commit to be in unity with all of them!

- The Table of the LORD is where we discover our place in the body. We discern the gifts the Holy Spirit has given us and how they fit in the context of the body. A healthy body is where every part functions at an optimal level for the benefit of all. Disconnected parts cannot survive. We must find our place and begin to function appropriately.

- The Table of the LORD is where we, as members of the body of Christ, renew and re-establish our connection with the Head, the Lord Jesus Christ. We are all connected to each other, and corporately connected to Him. The Head is where the brain is! We recognize our total dependence on Him for direction, instruction and inspiration. A body without a head is powerless.

- The Table of the LORD is where we can comprehend covenant from God's perspective and understand our part.

- The Table of the LORD is where we discover the One we serve is jealous and will not compete for our love and affection. Idolatry in any form is not tolerated at this Table and those who worship idols (anything we love more than God) and come to this Table will do so at their own peril. He will have first place or no place at all.

On February 15, when I returned home after work, my husband told me that he had just read something that I would definitely want to read. He took me to an email communication from James W. Goll, an internationally known prophetic voice for this generation. The following is the direct quote that confirmed to me that I was indeed hearing from the Holy Spirit regarding this subject of Communion. It confirmed I was on the right track!

It is taken from Goll's *Strategic Words for Our Day*, in the article entitled 5 Prophetic Insights for 2016, Point #4.

> **"'Communion, The Lord's Supper, is one of the highest and most overlooked weapons of spiritual warfare.'** This phrase was originally spoken to me years ago [1970's] when leading a prophetic intercessory group in Kansas City, MO. I wrote this line down in the front cover of my ASV Moody Bible.
>
> This past week [February/2016] as I was seeking the Lord for more understanding concerning an integrated healing model the Holy Spirit spoke this word to me again for the second time in my life. **'Communion, The Lord's Supper, is one of the highest and most overlooked weapons of spiritual warfare.'"** [208]

And then James Goll ended his statement speaking prophetically about the new way The Lord's Supper will be celebrated by those who are willing to hear God and make a break from tradition.

> "Old teachings will be made new on subjects such as The Power of the Blood, etc. As we partake in The Lord's Supper in congregational worship settings, the power of healing will break forth. We will cross over into the atmosphere of Divine Miracles where all things are possible." [209]

His words were signaling a radical change in Communion as we know it! *"Old teachings will be made new as we partake in The Lord's Supper* in CONGREGATIONAL WORSHIP SETTINGS!" He lists that as a precursor to miracles. How amazing is that?

The days our forefathers [in the 1600's through the 1800's] spent preparing to receive The Lord's Supper at the sacramental services were holy times, but would have been considered by them to be an absolute failure anytime the tangible Presence of the Spirit of God was absent from their Table. It was unthinkable! That is why they spent days seeking God, repenting and preparing themselves to partake of the meal together. They knew He would come and join them at the Table. They *knew* He would come. Do we have that same expectation as we partake of Communion while sitting in our pews?

That is exactly what we can (and should) expect each time we sit down at The Lord's Table with other believers. We certainly can expect the Presence of the Lord to join us. Just as it was for the children of Israel, this Table is a place of covenant renewal, and when we are serious about renewing our covenant to the Lord, He always comes. It is much like the vows of the covenant of marriage where both of those making covenant must attend. A wedding without the groom would be no wedding at all!

But for this to happen, it is imperative that revolutionary change must come in the way we celebrate this powerful sacramental event. The choice is not ours to make based on how we are comfortable celebrating it. Much like it was when He instituted the original Passover meal, the Lord can be very specific in how He wants His events to be celebrated. The choice belongs to Him, and it is great wisdom to pursue Him for His preferences.

I am not a prophet or the daughter of a prophet, but I believe this next declaration with every fiber of my being:

The Table of the LORD will be restored in our generation!

"Turn us back,
O God of our Deliverance/Salvation
and cause Your anger toward us to cease.
Will you be angry with us forever?
Will you draw out Your anger
To all generations?

Will you not revive us again
so Your people can rejoice in You?

Show us Your lovingkindness, LORD*,
And grant us Your salvation."

Psalm 85: 5-8
One New Man Bible

End Notes

[1] *The Great Awakening: The Roots of Evangelical Christianity in Colonial America*, Thomas S. Kidd, Yale University Press, 2009 (Wikipedia.org).

[2] *The Relationship Between Samuel J. Mills Jr. and the Influence of the Second Great Awakening on Missions and Evangelism*, Thomas H. Kiker, Dissertation and Thesis, Southeastern Baptist Theological Seminary, 2009.

[3] www.gospeltruth.net/revival200yearsago.htm.

[4] *Thy Kingdom Come: A Sketch of Christ's Church in Church History*, J. Parnell McCarter, as cited in *Worship through the Ages*, Towns and Whaley, p. 135.

[5] Ibid, p. 135.

[6] *The Ten Greatest Revivals Ever*, Elmer Towns & Douglas Porter, p. 73, as cited in *Worship through the Ages*, p. 135.

[7] Moody Magazine article, June 1986, by J. Edwin Orr, a leading scholar on revivals. Found on the website: http://www.villageschoolsofthebible.org/blog/the-second-great-awakening/

[8] *The Return of the Spirit*, and article on the following website, https://www.christianhistoryinstitute.org/magazine/article/return-of-the-spirit-second-great-awakening/

[9] Op cit., *Thy Kingdom Come*, cited in *Worship through the Ages*, p. 136

[10] http://classroom.synonym.com/areas-did-americans-settle-early-1800s-17751.html

[11] Article entitled *Prayer and Revival*, J. Edwin Orr, as cited on http://www.revival-library.org/catalogues/miscellanies/prayer/orr.html

[12] Op cit., www.gospeltruth.net/revival200yearsago.htm

[13] *Worship through the Ages: How the Great Awakenings Shape Evangelical Worship*, Elmer L. Towns & Vernon M. Whaley, 2012, B & H Publishing Company

[14] *The History of Methodism in Kentucky*, A. H. Redford (Albert Henry), 18-1884, p. 19.

[15] http://en.wikipedia.org/wiki/Revival_of_1800

[16] *The Role of Spiritual Awakening: How God Brought About (and Answered) The Concerts of Prayer of History*, An article by Dr. J. Edwin Orr, Campus Crusade for Christ, Intl., 1976.

[17] Ibid., *The Role of Spiritual Awakening*, Dr. J. Edwin Orr.

[18] *Revival at Cane Ridge*, Mark Galli, Christianity Today Magazine, 1995, Issue 45.

[19] *Tours into Kentucky and the Northwest Territory*, James Smith, p. 374, as cited in *The Great Revival: Beginnings of the Bible Belt*, John B. Boles, p. 26.

[20] *The Great Revival: Beginnings of the Bible Belt*, John B. Boles, The University Press of Kentucky, 1972, p. 50.

[21] Wilson to Reverend Samuel Wilson, Crowder's Creek, N.C., September 30, 1793, L. C. Glenn Collection, as cited in *The Great Revival: Beginnings of the Bible Belt*, John B. Boles, p. 42.

[22] *Sketches of North Carolina*, Foote, p. 376; and Caruthers, "Richard Hugg King," p. 40, as cited in *The Great Revival: Beginnings of the Bible Belt*, p. 42.

[23] *Tennessee: A History*, Wilma Dykeman, Wakestone Books Publishers, Nashville TN, 1993.

[24] Op cit., *Revival at Cane Ridge*, Mark Galli.

[25] Op cit., *Tennessee: A History*, p. 10.

[26] Op cit., *Tennessee: A History*, p. 16.

[27] Op cit., *Revival at Cane Ridge*, Mark Galli.

[28] *Founding of the Cumberland Settlements: The First Atlas, 1779–1804*, Doug Drake, Warioto Press, 2009.

[29] Op cit., *Tennessee: A History*, p. 17.

[30] Op cit., *Tennessee: A History*, p. 22.

[31] Western Missionary Magazine 1 (1803): 173, 177. (Excerpt from *Holy Fairs: Scotland and the Making of American Revivalism*, Leigh Eric Schmidt, 1989, Princeton University Press).

[32] *Holy Fairs: Scotland and the Making of American Revivalism*, Leigh Eric Schmidt, 1989, Princeton University Press.

[33] Ibid, *Holy Fairs*, p. 95.

[34] http://www.history.com/topics/martin-luther-and-the-95-theses

[35] http://spindleworks.com/library/aasman/lshowmany.htm

[36] Op cit., *Holy Fairs*, pp. 14, 15.

[37] Op cit., *Holy Fairs*, p. 15.

[38] Op cit., *Holy Fairs*, pp. 15, 18.

[39] *A Brief Historical Relation of the Life of Mr. John Livingston Minister of the Gospel*, John Livingston, as cited in *Holy Fairs: Scotland and the Making of American Revivalism*, p. 21.

[40] Op cit., *Holy Fairs*, p. 33.

[41] *Historical Collections*, p. 525-26, *Holy Fairs: Scotland and the Making of American Revivalism*, Leigh Eric Schmidt, p. 93.

[42] *The Great Revival in the West*, 1797-1805, Catharine Caroline Cleveland, 1916, University of Chicago Press, Chicago, IL, p. 52.

[43] *Forgotten Power: The Significance of the Lord's Supper in Revival*, William L. De Arteaga, Zondervan, Grand Rapids, Michigan, p. 217.

[44] Op. cit., *Worship through the Ages*, p. 135.

[45] *The Great Revival, 1787-1805: The Origins of the Southern Evangelical Mind*, John B. Boles, University Press of Kentucky, 1972, p. 91.

[46] *Early Times in Middle Tennessee*, John Carr, reprinted by Robert H. Horsley &

Assoc., 1958, Nashville, TN, Chapter 7.

[47] Op cit., *The Great Revival: Beginnings of the Bible Belt*, p. 41.

[48] http://www.cumberland.org/hfcpc/McGready.htm, Quote regarding Rev. McGready from Rev. John Andrews.

[49] *History of the Red River Meeting House*, Tom Ruley, article on the website-http://www.rrmh.org/history

[50] *Before the Great Awakening*, J. Edwin Orr, cited in *Worship through the Ages: How the Great Awakenings Shape Evangelical Worship*, Elmer L. Towns & Vernon M. Whaley, p. 141.

[51] Op cit., *The Great Revival: Beginnings of the Bible Belt*, p. 40.

[52] *Brief Biographical Sketches of some of the Early Ministers of the Cumberland Presbyterian Church*, Richard Beard, D.D. ,Nashville, TN, Southern Methodist Publishing House, 1867.

[53] *It Happened 200 Years Ago: The Great Revival*, an internet article cited on www.gospeltruth.net

[54] Op cit., *Brief Biological Sketches of some of the Early Ministers of the Cumberland Presbyterian Church*, p. 11.

[55] Op cit., *Before the Great Awakening*, J. Edwin Orr, cited in *Worship through the Ages: How the Great Awakenings Shape Evangelical Worship*, Elmer L. Towns & Vernon M. Whaley, p. 141.

[56] Op cit., *Brief Biological Sketches of some of the Early Ministers of the Cumberland Presbyterian Church*, p. 11.

[57] *The Life of Finis Ewing*, Cossit, pg. 43, as cited in *The Great Revival: Beginnings of the Bible Belt*, p. 40.

[58] *The Gasper River Meeting House*, Thomas Whitaker, an article found on the website, http://www.cumberland.org/hfcpc/churches/Whitaker.htm

[59] Op cit., *Brief Biological Sketches of some of the Early Ministers of the Cumberland Presbyterian Church*, p. 12.

[60] http://en.wikipedia.org/wiki/Revival_of_1800

[61] *The Great Revival in the West*, 1797-1805, Catharine Caroline Cleveland, 1916, University of Chicago Press, Chicago, IL, p. 45.

[62] *Church History in Plain Language*, Bruce L. Shelley, Word Publishing, 1982.

[63] *Revival Times in America*, Fred W. Hoffman, 1956, Published by W. A. Wilde Company.

[64] *Celebrating Sumner County's Bicentennial & Tennessee Homecoming '86*, An article that ran in the Religion section, The News-Examiner, Gallatin, March 29, 1986.

[65] *Legends of the War of Independence; and of the Earlier Settlements in the West*, T. Marshall Smith, J. F. Brennan Publisher, 1855, Chapter XXXVI, pp. 370, 371.

[66] Op cit., *The Great Revival in the West*, p. 45.

[67] Article entitled *Camp Meetings*, Conrad Ostwalt, as cited on http://tennesseeencyclopedia.net/entry.php?rec=179

[68] *Eighteenth Century Men of Zeal*, Paul A. Reardon, Published by lulu.com, p.90

[69] Ibid., *Eighteenth Century Men of Zeal*, (Boles 1976, 23-24), p. 90.

[70] Op cit., *Eighteenth Century Men of Zeal*, (Carr, Chap 7, p. 1), p. 88.

[71] Op cit., *Eighteenth Century Men of Zeal* (Carr, Chap 7, p. 1), p. 88.

[72] *Autobiography of Rev. James B. Finley; or Pioneer Life in the West*, William P. Strickland, Cincinnati, OH, 1856.

[73] *A Religious History of the American People*, Sydney E. Ahlstrom, David D. Hall, Yale University Press, 2004.

[74] *Early Times in Middle Tennessee*, John Carr, Nashville, TN, 1857, Stephenson & Owen Publishing.

[75] Article entitled *Camp Meeting* as cited on https://tennesseeencyclopedia.net/entry.php?rec=1270

[76] Op cit., *Early Times in Middle Tennessee*, John Carr, Nashville, TN, 1857, Stephenson & Owen Publishing.

[77] *Francis Asbury*, L. C. Rudolph, Nashville, 1966.

[78] Op cit., *An Endless Line of Splendor: Revivals and Their Leaders to the Great Awakening to Present*, p. 95.

[79] *Witness to Expansion: Bishop Francis Asbury on the Trans-Appalachian Frontier*, The Register of the Kentucky Historical Society, Copyright/1984, p. 335.

[80] Ibid, *Witness to Expansion*, p. 343.

[81] Op cit., (Filson 333, 335), cited in *Eighteenth Century Men of Zeal*, p.45.

[82] Op cit., *Early Times in Middle Tennessee*, John Carr, p. 47

[83] *America's Bishop: The Life of Francis Asbury*, Quote from Darius L. Salter's book, as cited on this website- http://www.imarc.cc/buletins/asburyq.html

[84] https://www.christianhistoryinstitute.org/magazine/article/knock-em-down-preachers/

[85] As cited on, http://www.ushistory.org/us/22c.asp

[86] Op Cit., *An Endless Line of Splendor: Revivals and Their Leaders to the Great Awakening to Present*, Earle Edwin Cairns, WIPF & Stock Publishers, p. 98.

[87] Op cit., *Eighteenth Century Men of Zeal*, (Carr, chapter 10), p. 41.

[88] Op cit., *Eighteenth Century Men of Zeal*, (Stone quote, Chapter 5), p. 42.

[89] *American Hymns Old and New*. Christ-Janer, Albert, Charles W. Hughes, and Carleton Sprague Smith. New York: Columbia University Press, 1980, p.380.

[90] *The American Republic: A Nation of Christians*, Paul R. Dienstberger, Chapt. 4.

[91] Op cit., *Firefall*, page 237, as cited on http://www.prdienstberger.com/nation/atbofcon.htm

[92] Op cit., *An Endless Line of Splendor: Revivals and Their Leaders to the Great Awakening to Present*, p. 100.

[93] *The Story of Christianity, Vol. 2: The Reformation to the Present Day*, Justo L. Gonzales, New York: Harper One, 1984, pp. 245 – 246.

[94] Article entitled, *Camp Meetings*, as cited on http://digitalheritage.org/2010/08/camp-meetings/

[95] *A Short Narrative of Revival*, James McGready, p. 154.

[96] Op cit., *Revival at Cane Ridge*, Mark Galli, p. 4.

[97] Op cit., *A Religious History of the American People*, p. 434, 435.

[98] Op cit., http://en.wikipedia.org/wiki/Revival_of_1800

[99] Op cit., *Early Times in Middle Tennessee*, p. 79.

[100] Op cit., *Holy Fairs: Scotland and the Making of American Revivalism*, Leigh Eric Schmidt, p. 169.

[101] Ibid., *Holy Fairs,* p. 169.

[102] Article entitled *History of the Red River Meeting,* as cited on http://www.rrmh.org/history

[103] *Narrative of the Commencement…of the Revival*, James McGready, p. xi, as cited in *The Great Revival: Beginnings of the Bible Belt*, p. 49.

[103] Op cit., *Legends of the War of Independence*, CHAPTER XXXVI, p. 370.

[104] Op cit., *The American Republic: A Nation of Christians*, as cited on http://www.prdienstberger.com/nation/atbofcon.htm

[105] Op cit., *Legends of the War of Independence*, CHAPTER XXXVI, p. 370.

[106] Op cit., www.gospeltruth.net/revival200yearsago.htm

[107] Op cit., *The Ten Greatest Revivals Ever*, Porter and Towns, p. 79, as cited in *Worship through the Ages*, p. 141-142.

[108] Op cit., *The Gasper River Meeting House*, Thomas Whitaker.

[109] *History of Tennessee*, The Goodspeed Publishing Co.: Nashville, 1886, p.650.

[110] Op Cit., *Celebrating Sumner County's Bicentennial & Tennessee Homecoming '86*

[111] *Legends of the War of Independence*, Thomas Marshall Smith, Published by The British Library, p. 374.

[112] http://www.cumberland.org/hfcpc/churches/BeechTN.htm

[113] Op cit., *The Gasper River Meeting House*, Thomas Whitaker.

[114] Op cit., *The Gasper River Meeting House*, Thomas Whitaker.

[115] *The Great Revival of 1800*, William Speer, D.D., 1872, Presbyterian Board of Education, Philadelphia, pp. 40-42.

[116] Op cit., *The Gasper River Meeting House*, Thomas Whitaker.

[117] Op cit., *The Gasper River Meeting House*, Thomas Whitaker.

[118] Op cit., *The Return of the Spirit*, www.christianhistoryinstitute.org

[119] Op cit., *The Great Revival of 1800*, p. 40.

[120] *The Frontier Camp Meeting: Religion's Harvest Time*, Charles A. Johnson, pp. 34, 36, as cited on the internet article, *The Camp Meeting on the Frontier and the Methodist Religious Resort in the East–Before 1900*, Charles A. Parker, archives.gcah.org

[121] An internet article entitled, *It Happened 200 Years Ago: The Great Revival,* cited on www.gospeltruth.net

[122] *A Short Narrative of the Revival*, McGready, p. 153, as cited in *The Great Revival: Beginnings of the Bible Belt*, p. 49.

[123] *Autobiographical Sketch*, John Rankin, p. 279, as cited in *The Great Revival:*

Beginnings of the Bible Belt, p. 49.

[124] Op cit., *History of Tennessee*, p. 650.

[125] *The Great Leap Westward: A History of Sumner County, Tennessee*, Walter T. Durham, 1969, Publisher: Sumner County Public Library Board, Gallatin TN.

[126] Op cit., *Early Times in Middle Tennessee*, John Carr, Chapter 7.

[127] *Historic Rock Castle: A History of Hendersonville and the Surrounding Area*, Mrs. Willie McGee Ellis.

[128] http://www.findagrave.com/cgi-bin/fg.cgi?page=cr&CRid=1554765

[129] Article entitled *Camp Meetings*, as cited on-https://tennesseeencyclopedia.net/entry.php?rec=179

[130] Op cit., *The Great Leap Westward*, pp. 165, 166.

[131] *Reverend Francis Asbury's Journal*, Francis Asbury, 1800, p. 396.

[132] *A Pictorial History of Sumner County Tennessee: 1786 – 1986*, Walter T. Durham & James W. Thomas, Sumner County Historical Society, 1986.

[133] Op cit., *Witness to Expansion*, pp. 344-345.

[134] Article entitled *Richard Whatcoat: An Example of Perfect Love*, compiled by Duane V. Maxey, p. 13, as cited on http://wesley.nnu.edu/wesleyctr/books/0601-0700/HDM0610.pdf

[135] *Reverend Francis Asbury's Journal*, Francis Asbury, 1800, p. 396-397.

[136] Op cit., *Eighteenth Century Men of Zeal: Passion among Kentucky Tennessee Frontier*, p. 92.

[137] http://www.cumberland.org/hfcpc/churches/RidgeTN.htm

[138] Op cit., *The Gasper River Meeting House*, Thomas Whitaker.

[139] Op cit., *The Great Revival in the West*, 1797-1805, p. 64.

[140] http://www.geni.com/people/William-McGee/6000000010764451633

[141] *The Posthumous Works of James McGready*, p. xi ADD other Info http://www.cumberland.org/hfcpc/churches/RidgeTN.htm

[142] Op cit., www.cumberland.org/hfcpc/churches/RidgeTN.htm

[143] http://www.rootsweb.ancestry.com/~tnsumner/sumnsh1.htm

[144] http://www.geni.com/people/William-McGee/6000000010764451633

[145] Op cit., *The Gasper River Meeting House*, Thomas Whitaker.

[146] Op cit, *The Great Leap Westward*, pp. 166, 167.

[147] Op cit., *A Pictorial History of Sumner County Tennessee*, p. 116.

[148] Op cit., *Early Times in Middle Tennessee*, Chapter 7.

[149] Op cit., *Eighteenth Century Men of Zeal: Passion among Kentucky Tennessee Frontier*, p.92.

[150] http://www.mansker.org/history/durham.htm

[151] *Isaac Walton, 1794-1840, Volume One: The Walton Family*, Robert Polk Thomson, Sumner County Historical Archive, 2005.

[152] *The Night Writers of Watkins Institute: The Third Stanza of Their Song*, Article, Sumner County Historical Archives.

[153] http://www.mansker.org/photos/statpic20.htm, documenting a historical

marker in honor of both Isaac Walton and Casper Mansker in Goodlettsville, TN

[154] https://ccountz.wordpress.com/page/2/

[155] http://www.rootsweb.ancestry.com/~tnsumner/walton2.htm Webpage on Isaac Walton's descendants, contributed by Connie Moretti.

[156] *The Upper Cumberland of Pioneer Times*, Alvin B. Wirt, as cited on the following website- http://www.ajlambert.com/history/hst_ucpt.pdf

[157] Op cit., *Worship through the Ages*, Townes and Whaley, p. 142.

[158] Op cit., *The Return of the Spirit*, www.christianhistoryinstitute.org

[159] Op cit., *A Religious History of the American People*, Sydney E. Ahlstrom, 1972, Vail-Ballou Press, Binghamton, NY.

[160] *Account of the Work of God*, Armenius, p. 273.

[161] Op cit., *Revival at Cane Ridge*, Mark Galli, p.5.

[162] Op cit., *Revival at Cane Ridge*, Mark Galli, p.5.

[163] Op cit., *Revival Times in America*, p. 77.

[164] Op cit., *The Return of the Spirit*, www.christianhistoryinstitute.org

[165] Op cit., *Revival at Cane Ridge*, Mark Galli, p. 3.

[166] Op cit., *The Night Writers of Watkins Institute*, pp. 4, 5.

[167] Op cit., *Early Times in Middle Tennessee*, pp. 36.

[168] Op cit., *Early Times in Middle Tennessee*, pp. 37 – 38.

[169] Op cit., *Early Times in Middle Tennessee*, pp. 38.

[170] *Autobiography of Peter Cartwright: The Backwoods Preacher*, Peter Cartwright, edited by W. P. Strickland, New York, Carlton & Porter, 1857.

[171] *The Story of Christian Music: From Gregorian Chant to Black Gospel*, Andrew Wilson-Dickson, Minneapolis: Fortress Press, 1992, p. 192 (Quoted in *Worship through the Ages*).

[172] Works, vii-xi; *Western Magazine* 1 (1803), James McGready, as cite in *Holy Fairs: Scotland and the Making of American Revivalism*, Leigh Eric Schmidt.

[173] http://www.godsgenerals.com/person_james_mc.htm

[174] Op cit., *The Gasper River Meeting House*, Thomas Whitaker.

[175] http://www.whatcoat.com/WhoWasWhatcoat.htm

[176] Op cit., *Forgotten Power: The Significance of the Lord's Supper in Revival*, p. 270.

[177] Op cit., *The Return of the Spirit*, www.christianhistoryinstitute.org

[178] Op cit., *The Great Revival, 1787-1805: The Origins of the Southern Evangelical Mind*, John B. Boles.

[179] Op cit., *Revival Times in America*, pp. 77-78.

[180] Op cit., *Early Times in Middle Tennessee*, Chapter 7.

[181] *The Second Great Awakening, Part 2*, (website article), Jay Guin, http://www.sullivan-county.com/immigration/2nd_awakening.htm

[182] *Eighteenth Century Men of Zeal*, p. 92.

[183] Op cit., *The American Republic: A Nation of Christians*.

[184] *A Tennessee Chronicle*, Cartter Patten, 1953, Printed in USA.

[185] As cited on the following website-
http://www.firstprescookeville.org/Publications/HistoryofCkvlFPC/Presby
HistoryChapter1.pdf
[186] Op cit., *Worship through the Ages*, p.154.
[187] http://www.christianity.com/church/church-history/timeline/1701-
1800/the-2nd-great-awakening-11630336.html
[188] Op cit., *The Second Great Awakening*, Part 2.
[189] https://en.wikipedia.org/wiki/Sacred_Harp
[190] *The Story of Christian Music*, Wilson-Dickson, p. 193, as cited in *Worship through the Ages*, p.152.
[191] *History of the Christian Church: From its Origin to the Present Time*, James Smith.
[192] Op cit., *Camp Meeting* article, Conrad Ostwalt.
[193] Op cit., Camp Meeting article, Conrad Ostwalt.
[194] Op cit., *The Great Revival, 1787-1805: The Origins of the Southern Evangelical Mind*, John B. Boles, p. 91.
[195] Op cit., *History of Tennessee*, p. 78.
[196] Op cit., *Autobiography of Peter Cartwright*, p. 4.
[197] Op cit., *Eighteenth Century Men of Zeal*, (Carr, Chapter 7, p. 1), p. 88.
[198] Op cit., *A Pictorial History of Sumner County Tennessee*, p. 116.
[199] *Life and Times of Rev. John Brooks*, Rev. John Brooks & Learner Blackman, Published at the Nashville Christian Advocate Office, 1848.
[200] Op cit, www.gospeltruth.net/revival200yearsago.html
[201] Op cit., *Early Times in Middle Tennessee*.
[202] Op cit., *Early Times in Middle Tennessee*.
[203] Op cit, *Camp Meeting* article, Conrad Ostwalt.
[204] Op cit, www.gospeltruth.net/revival200yearsago.html
[205] Op cit., www.gospeltruth.net/revival200yearsago.htm
[206] Op cit., www.gospeltruth.net/revival200yearsago.htm
[207] Quote from William J. Morford, translator of the *One New Man Bible*.
[208] *5 Prophetic Insights for 2016*, James W. Goll, found on the website:
www.jimgoll.com/Communications/StrategicWordsForOurDay/tabid/1351/ArticleId/217/Default.aspx
[209] Ibid, *5 Prophetic Insights for 2016*, James W. Goll.

60499077R00121

Made in the USA
Charleston, SC
01 September 2016